HELPERS AND AIDES

by
Irene M. Franck
and
David M. Brownstone

**A Volume in the Work Throughout History
Series**

A Hudson Group Book

Facts On File Publications
New York, New York • Oxford, England

Helpers and Aides

First published in the United States of America by Facts On File, Inc.
460 Park Avenue South, New York, New York 10016.

1089 BKF FOL 13.26

Library of Congress Cataloging-in-Publication Data

Franck, Irene M.
  Helpers and aides.

11/13 FOL 1500

  (Work throughout history)
  "Hudson Group book."
  Bibliography: p.
  Includes index.
  Summary: Explores the role throughout history of helping professions,
including drivers, exterminators, firefighters, social workers, and others.
    1. Occupations—History—Juvenile literature.
[1. Occupations—History] I. Brownstone, David M.
II. Title. III. Series.
HF5381.2.F68 1987 331.7 86-24370
ISBN 0-8160-1445-0

British Library CIP Data available

Printed in the United States of America

10 9 8 7 6 5 4 3 2 1

Contents

Preface v

Introduction vii

Bath Workers 1

Child Nurses 9

Drivers 23

Exterminators and Pest Controllers 47

Firefighters 51

Launderers 59

Matchmakers 63

Movers 73

Private Guards and Detectives 89

Sanitation Workers 93

Servants and Other Domestic Laborers 107

Social Workers 133

Undertakers 147

Suggestions for Further Reading 173

Index 178

Preface

Helpers and Aides is a book in the multi-volume series, *Work Throughout History*. Work shapes the lives of all human beings; yet surprisingly little has been written about the history of the many fascinating and diverse types of occupations men and women pursue. The books in the *Work Throughout History* series explore humanity's most interesting, important, and influential occupations. They explain how and why these occupations came into being in the major cultures of the world, how they evolved over centuries, especially with changing technology, and how society's view of each occupation has changed. Throughout we focus on what it was like to do a particular kind of work—for example, to be a farmer, glassblower, midwife, banker, building contractor, actor, astrologer, or weaver—in centuries past and right up to today. Because many occupations have been closely related to one another, we have included at the end of each article references to other overlapping occupations. In preparing this series, we have drawn on a wide range of general works on social, economic, and occupational history, including many on everyday life throughout history. We consulted far too many wide-ranging works to list them all here; but at the end of each volume is a list of suggestions for further reading, should readers want to learn more about any of the occupations included in the volume.

Many researchers and writers worked on the preparation of this series. For *Helpers and Aides*, the primary researcher-writer was David G. Merrill; Thomas Crippen also worked on part of this work. Our thanks go to them for their fine work; to our expert typists, Shirley Fenn, Nancy Fishelberg, and Mary Racette; to our most helpful editors at Facts On File, first Kate Kelly and then James Warren, and their assistant Claire Johnston; to our excellent developmental editor, Vicki Tyler; and to our publisher, Edward Knappman, who first suggested the *Work Through History* series and has given us gracious support during the long years of its preparation.

Irene M. Franck
David M. Brownstone

Introduction

Throughout history, people have employed others to do jobs that they were unwilling or unable to do for themselves. The workers who did these jobs have been the *helpers* and *aides* of this world.

For many thousands of years and in many different cultures, the babies of wealthy or even modestly comfortable families were put into the care of *child nurses* for many months, often for as long as five years. These women nursed, fed, dressed, taught, and in all respects cared for the child in place of the mother. Sometimes the child lived in the nurse's home, perhaps with other children; otherwise the nurse would leave her own home and family to care for the baby in her employer's home.

In the home itself, *servants* and other *domestic laborers* of all sorts performed all the jobs that, in a poorer home, would be done by the family members. From *butlers* and *maids* to *chancellors* and *stewards*, from *grooms* and *ushers* to *pantlers* and *chamberlains*, the houses of the wealthy teemed with specialists, each carrying out specific functions in the running of a major household. Very large households would sometimes employ their own *launderers*. But very often launderers worked independently, either "taking in washing" or working in a shop that did washing—and in modern times dry cleaning—for many people.

When the children of a family grew to adulthood, a *matchmaker* was often called in to arrange a suitable marriage. In Europe, this practice was most common among rich or noble families. But in the East, matchmakers of some sort were employed by even the poorest of families, if only because they had to consult the horoscopes of the proposed couple to see if they were favorable for the marriage. In Western countries today, individuals often consult organizations, many of which use computers, to match people for dating, if not necessarily for marriage.

In the days when water was not freely available in most homes, many people went to bath houses to wash and relax. There *bath workers* watched their belongings, fetched refreshments, and provided whatever other such services they required. In modern times, many of these people are skilled assistants in clubs that offer not only pools and saunas but also equipment for physical fitness.

Families who have fallen on hard times can—at least in modern times—call on the services of the *social worker*. Although charity has a long history in human societies, social workers as professional helpers have been on the scene only since the 19th century.

At death, different specialists were called in: the *undertakers*. In countries where funerals grew elaborate, these people were called in to oversee the arrangements, from the preparation of the body to the final handling, such as burial or cremation.

Many other helpers and aides provided more general services to the public at large. *Drivers* were employed from early times to handle load-bearing animals and any vehicles such as carts or wagons that they pulled. In modern times drivers are employed in all forms of land transportation, from trucks and buses to trains and automobiles. Their counterparts, *ferriers* and *boat operators*, provide similar services in all forms of water transport.

Movers provide a different kind of transport service, hauling heavy loads in places where vehicles and load-bearing animals are not used. For much of history movers have relied primarily on their own strength to do their work; only in recent centuries have they had much in the way of machinery to make their tasks easier.

In the long centuries before modern *police* forces were developed, many people relied on *private guards* and *detectives* to safeguard themselves and their property. Today such people are still often employed on a private basis to obtain information or to guard premises.

In cities and towns built of wood or other flammable materials, fire has always been a dreaded hazard; at its worst a fire may destroy much of a city. But for most of history it was left to people themselves, informally, to fight whatever fires occurred. Not until recent centuries, and then only in the large cities, have there been professional *firefighters* to help save settlements and forests from destruction by fire.

In country or city, people have always had to battle against pests such as rats, cockroaches, or wild dogs. They have often employed professional *exterminators* or *pest controllers* to help rid the area of such pests. In cities and especially on ships, where rodents could do much damage to precious stores, *rat catchers* were often employed. Modern exterminators and pest controllers rely heavily on chemicals to do their work.

Crowded cities, especially in modern times, have also generated a great deal of garbage. This is not only un-sightly but is also a breeding place for pests and disease, so it must be cleared away. The people who, in modern times, have taken on the job of keeping cities and towns clean are the *sanitation workers*.

Today, with work-saving appliances such as washing machines and vacuum cleaners, most people are less reliant on helpers and aides in the home. But as people are increasingly drawn to live in crowded cities and suburbs, helpers and aides play ever more important roles in the public areas of our lives.

Bath Workers

Bath workers supervise and assist people in public bathing and related activities. Public baths existed in ancient Mohenjo-Daro in the Indus Valley, and later on the island of Crete. The ancient Greeks were one of the earliest peoples truly concerned about physical hygiene. They had established public baths for health purposes by the fifth century B.C. Initially, only cold water was used, to prevent the baths from becoming mere social centers of relaxation, idleness, and gossip. The Greek bath eventually became a part of a larger concept—the *gymnasium*—where *philosophers* held symposiums and lectures, *athletes* trained, and citizens exercised, walked, and enjoyed both warm and cold baths.

The Romans had a similar institution—the *thermae*—which usually included *palaestrae* (recreation and exercise rooms). The Romans popularized the concept of public bathing more than any other people before or after them. By the fourth century A.D., there were some 1,000 public baths in Rome alone, and many others in outlying districts of the Empire, including Britain, where the city of Bath was founded in those days. The baths were usually quite affordable, and most citizens attended them quite regularly. Upper-class people were usually accompanied by a personal slave or two, who gave them massages and perfume rubs. (The Greeks had been especially fond of olive oil anointments.) Other less affluent people paid a small fee for such services, done by *masseurs*, *anointers*, *perfumers*, and *depilators* (who removed unwanted body hair); many of these were also slaves, employed by the *bath operators*. Special *elaeothesia* (massage and anointing rooms) were reserved for this purpose.

Roman baths could be either both privately or publicly owned and operated. They were run much like modern-day swimming pools, except that bathing was done in the nude. Later in the Empire, mixed bathing (men and women together) was common. Many moralists and even some emperors criticized the practice and Hadrian once banned it, but nudity seemed to be no great concern for the most part. Rulers were known to bathe in the same pools with peasants, men with women, children with adults. Bathing was seen not only as recreational, but also as hygienic. Pliny once noted—with considerable exaggeration—that medicine had not been needed in Rome for centuries because of the common practice of bathing. Medicinal *spas* and *hot springs* were also popular in Greece and Rome, and many of that time are still in operation today.

Bathing was not all healthy and relaxing, though. *Bath attendants*—either slaves or servants—were notorious *thieves*. Many people returned to the dressing rooms to find their valuables missing, or fine garments replaced by old and worn ones. This annoyance became so severe that a law was finally enacted making stealing from a public bath a capital offense (one punishable by death). Although public baths in Rome had, at first, been visited mostly by the lower classes, they quickly became a favorite of everyone. At the same time, though, they also became favorite haunts for *prostitutes*, and many all-night bath establishments were well-known for the promiscuous activities they promoted.

After the fall of the Roman Empire, public baths never again regained their prominence in Western Europe. They actually fell into disuse for hundreds of years, and did not reappear in Europe until around the 12th century A.D. Some continued in the Eastern Roman Empire, however.

The Moslems had the most advanced system of public baths for many centuries. The *hammam* was the most common type of public bath in the East. It was often owned and operated by wealthy individuals who profited greatly from the universal appeal of baths. Moorish Spain was a great center for these baths. There were several hundred at one time in the city of Córdoba alone. A modified version of the *hammam* still survives today as the popular "Turkish bath." In northern Europe Russian vapor baths and Finnish saunas were popular.

Around the 15th century, bathing was revived with a flurry in Western Europe. Baths were strongly—but in vain—condemned by both Reformation and Catholic preachers because they featured mixed bathing in the nude, and private steam cabins, tubs, and beds. Good music, food, and wine were an integral part of the activity surrounding these places, which became centers for socializing and prostitution much more than for healthful exercising, hygiene and therapy, as they had been earlier. The *stews*, as European bathhouses were first called, became nothing but brothels and common breeding grounds for syphilis and other venereal diseases by the 16th century. Their owners and operators, often called *bathers*, were counted by many as being among the most despicable characters in the world. Bathing in general—public or private—had a rather poor public

Bathhouse proprietors washed, bled, massaged, and deloused their patrons, men and women alike. (By Jost Amman, from The Book of Trades, *late 16th century)*

image. We are told, for example, that Queen Elizabeth bathed once a month (privately) "whether she required it or not."

Public baths continued in operation in Eastern Europe even into the 17th and 18th centuries, while in the West they had largely disappeared once more. One exception was bathing for therapy and hygiene supervised by a group of Parisian *barber-surgeons* into the 17th century. By 1800 there were hardly any public baths in the Western world, although they remained very popular in Japan, China, and the Islamic world. In France only a handful of luxury "Chinese baths" were operated aboard resort ships that cruised the Seine River. Moreover, few Westerners bathed more than once or twice a year, even in private.

The second half of the 19th century saw a marked change in this situation. New insight into the health value of cleanliness and personal hygiene made mineral baths, hot springs, and spas newly appreciated. Their operators catered to the elite classes, reaching their heyday in Victorian England when they offered fine dining and recreation along with bathing and massaging to their weekend and holiday visitors. As industrialization brought increasing leisure time to the rich and comfortable, the guest lists lengthened considerably. *Masseurs* and *masseuses* began to receive special training, as they had for years in Japan. Public swimming—bathers being dressed in sporty attire—also became popular around this time, although many social

With swimming a popular pastime, the lifeguard became a much-needed specialist. (By J. Durkin, from Frank Leslie's, *August 24, 1889)*

critics were shocked to see women outdoors in what was, for the time, skimpy clothing.

As swimming continued to gain in popularity in the 20th century, specially trained *lifeguards* were employed to protect people from drowning. After the 1930's, spas and health resorts began to tail off in popularity. In the 1970's and 1980's, there has been a revival of business for health resorts, especially those catering to people wishing to lose weight. Massage is important in such cases not only for pleasure but as a therapy for reducing stress. Some masseuses and masseurs receive special training in techniques such as Oriental *shiatsu*. Hydrotherapy (water therapy) has come out of the natural hygienic movement, as have other therapies designed to cleanse inner organs. Many competent and specially trained people work in these areas, but in the absence of licensing procedures, many novices and even outright charlatans have also been known to practice these arts.

Lifeguards received increasingly strict and formal training after the 1920's, as swimming became a widely popular sport. Gymnasiums also began to be popular as establishments designed especially for exercising, although baths and saunas have continued to be part of them. Such places employ special instructors for athletic activities as well as for exercise and diet regulation, as do their more recent offshoots—racquet clubs, indoor tennis halls, and diet and exercise studios.

Public baths were revived in the United States in the early 20th century, partly because of the arrival of many Eastern European immigrants who were used to them. In recent decades they have become strongly associated with male homosexual activity. Massage parlors, meanwhile, have almost become synonymous with brothels, for which they are often thinly veiled fronts. Reputable masseurs and masseuses are usually licensed and work in legitimate health clubs and gymnasiums. Some of them work privately for individuals such as athletes, boxers, or business executives; athletic trainers also perform this service.

For related occupations in other volumes of the series, see the following:

in *Builders*
    Plumbers
in *Healers* (forthcoming):
    Barbers
    Nurses
    Physicians and Surgeons
in *Performers and Players* (forthcoming):
    Athletes
    Athletic Coaches and Trainers
in *Scholars and Priests* (forthcoming):
    Scholars
in *Warriors and Adventurers* (forthcoming):
    Prostitutes
    Robbers and Other Criminals

Child Nurses

The special task of caring for and raising children from infancy to school or working age has traditionally fallen to the *wet nurse*. She was capable of breast-feeding a baby (often along with a child of her own) when the natural mother was either unable or unwilling to do so. She performed her nursing chores for fees or favors, either at her own home or in that of the natural mother, who would usually provide her with room and board in addition to other considerations. Although theirs was an ancient occupation, wet nurses were not numerous, for only upper-class mothers could afford the luxury. Still, professional wet nurses were important enough for laws to be made regulating their fees and practice. Babylonian nurses could have their breasts cut off if they substituted one child for another, or if a baby in their care died.

Wet nursing was not widely popular in Greco-Roman times. The advice of the second century A.D. physician, Soranus of Ephesus, seems to indicate the general view: ". . . it is better to feed the child with maternal milk . . . . But if anything prevents it one must choose the best wet nurse." Wet nurses were often recommended by *midwives*, who assisted at the births of the children. Royalty and aristocratic women typically used slaves or *housemaids* as wet nurses. For many centuries, especially after the fall of the Roman Empire, relatively few people demanded the services of professional wet nurses. Not until the end of the Middle Ages did demand rise sufficiently for wet nursing to be considered a major occupation.

The European Commercial Revolution in the 16th century brought a new middle class to the West. The result was something new in history. Greater numbers of people than ever before could be counted among the rich, well-to-do, or "comfortable." The demand for luxuries reached a new high—including a demand for wet nurses. Middle- and upper-class women clamored to imitate court society, and court ladies and gentlewomen found it ever more difficult to obtain slaves or even acceptable housemaids for this very special undertaking. Wet nursing, then, from that time until World War II, became a thriving profession, one that still lingers in many of the underdeveloped nations of the world.

From at least the 14th century A.D., middle-class families in Italy took great care in selecting proper wet nurses or *balia*. Newborn children were generally sent away to be raised and nourished by strangers for anywhere from one to five years; they were delivered to wet nurses right after birth and seem to have been kept for an average of two years. A 14th-century moralist listed these requirements for a good wet nurse: "She should be prudent, well-mannered, honest, not a drinker or a drunkard, because very often children draw from and resemble the nature of the milk they suck; and therefore be careful the wet nurses of your children aren't proud and don't have other evil traits." Many feared surrendering their children to what the preacher San Bernardino of Siena called "a dirty drab" from whom the baby might absorb evil customs while it "sucked her polluted blood."

The demand for wet nurses continued to grow, increasing proportionately with social status and wealth. Unfortunately wet nurses were notoriously slack in their care of taken-in babies. And even if they were diligent and sincere, the baby was still widely thought to imbibe a peasant woman's values and even physical characteristics while sucking her milk. Families who wanted their children raised as well as possible, therefore, had to search far and wide for appropriate, decent, relatively well-bred, healthy wet nurses—a search in which few were successful. Alberti, an Italian Renaissance writer, charged the father with this duty:

> He must think far ahead to find a good nurse, he must . . . get hold of one who will be ready in time. He must check that she is not sick or of immoral character . . . . Yet this sort of person always seems to be unavailable just when you need her most . . . . You know, too, how rare is a good nurse and how much in demand.

At about the same time, a merchant named Datini even acted as an *agent* in helping couples find suitable nurses. It was not an enviable task, however; he himself once wrote that decent *balia* "seem to have vanished from the world for none has come into my hands." Other agents in the business were *slave owners*, who sold or leased nurses. These slaves were considered generally undesirable as nurses for fine folk, but many *espedali* (orphanages) willingly dealt with slave owners. Household slaves and *servants* were also tried for this job, but they were usually considered unsuitable for the task, or were too overworked in their household duties to perform this special service to the liking of their masters.

Peasant women turned out to be the best source of wet nurses. Their husbands were usually eager for them to seek out extra income in this way, and sometimes forced them to undertake wet nursing. Sometimes wet nurses might even be taken in to live with a royal or noble family. This was an expensive undertaking, but the wealthiest and most particular clients were willing to suffer it for the sake of being absolutely sure that the wet nurse was not engaging in sexual activities, and thereby (as was believed then) endangering the life and morals of the baby. A household wet nurse was obliged to virtually sever all contacts with her husband or any other man during her years of service. King Henry IV of France was said to have fired one of the live-in nurses he employed after she was caught merely speaking with her husband.

Peasant women like this one dancing often acted as wet nurses, either taking the child home or living with the child in its family's great house. (By Albrecht Dürer, 1514)

By the 17th century the use of wet nurses was beginning to come under attack from clerics, social critics, and others. Most of this early criticism came from England, where the business of wet nursing was sharply curtailed long before it was even viewed as suspect in Germany, France, or elsewhere. By 1596 the Countess of Lincoln had already written a book admonishing mothers to do their own nursing for the good of their children and of England's family-oriented culture. The tombstone of the second wife of the Earl of Manchester had this eulogy etched upon its surface in 1658: "she nursed with her own breasts . . . . Her children shall rise up and call her blessed."

There were various reasons for the declining reliance upon wet nurses. One was that noble families found it increasingly distasteful to employ peasant women they considered crude to care for their prized offspring, who were to carry on fine family traditions. At the root of this distaste was the long-held fear that the child would absorb—directly through the nurse's milk—unbecoming personalities and poor health. Of course, the belief had a favorable side. In the late 15th and early 16th centuries, Michelangelo was fond of noting how his skill in sculpture had been derived from the blood of his wet nurse—the wife of a stone-cutter. The woman was so dear to his memory that he considered her not only his first inspiration, but in many ways, his actual mother. "With my mother's milk," he told a friend, in speaking of her, "I sucked in the hammer and chisels I use for my statues."

Another factor in the declining use of wet nurses was the increasing amount of talk about the joys and satisfactions of nursing. The French *obstetrician*, François Mauriceau, spoke about the "mutual agreement of tempers" that naturally bonded mother and child, making the natural mother the most suitable nurse. Another French doctor, Laurent Joubert, insisted: "If women only knew the joys of nursing they would not only not forego it with their own—they would hire themselves out."

The most decisive factor in the decline of this once-thriving profession was the actual care that "put-out" babies received from mercenary wet nurses. Many nurses took in more than one baby at a time, and some ran regular boarding houses for them. This must have meant rather good earnings, for we know that wet nurses in London were earning 25 pounds a year by the middle of the 18th century—a very tidy sum for those times. The number of babies a nurse took in was undoubtedly a factor in the negotiation of her fees, but many nurses were less than honest in divulging such information. At least a few of them maintained several different locations for their operations to conceal how many babies they had taken in. When too many babies were taken in by one nurse, the obvious danger was that they would suffer not only from neglect, but also from malnutrition and perhaps outright physical abuse from the overworked nurse.

Neglect, abuse, and simple mishandling of babies was widespread, regardless of how many babies were in a wet nurse's care. They were typically swaddled tightly in blankets and bedclothing to keep them from crying or thrashing about. Sometimes they were so tightly swaddled, and for so long at a time, that they became crippled, deformed, stunted in growth—and at times even lapsed into comas and died. Many nurses handled infants' restlessness and crying with liberal doses of both opium and liquor. A certain Dr. Hume blamed wet nurses for the high infant mortality rate of his time. Writing in 1799, he claimed that many of them were guilty of little short of murdering those infants left in their care, as they were "forever pouring Godfrey's Cordial down their little throats, which is a strong opiate and in the end as fatal as arsenic. This they pretend they do to quiet the child—thus indeed many are forever quieted . . . ." Liquor, too, he continued, was constantly being "poured down the throat of a little being who is incapable of declining the portion, but who exhibits an abhorrence by struggling efforts and wry faces . . . ." A little earlier than this, in 1757, even stronger words had been used against the profession by another observer:

> In and about London a prodigious number of children are cruelly murdered by those infernals called nurses. These infernal monsters throw a spoonful of gin, spirits of wine or Hungary water down a child's throat, which instantly strangles the babe. When the searchers come to inspect the body, and inquire what distemper caused the death, it is answered, "convulsions." This occasions the articles of convulsions in the Bills so much to exceed all others.

These charges against wet nurses were not new. In the 17th century a country rector noted that his parish had once been filled with suckling infants from London and yet, in the space of one year, he buried them all except two." By 1748 Dr. William Cadogan, in his *Essay Upon Nursing and the Management of Children*, claimed that nine out of ten babies put out to wet nurses died from lack of proper attention and care as well as from contaminated milk. He drew the ironical conclusion that the poorer the family to which a baby was born, the better its chances for survival and normal health. In 1774 an English gentleman, John G. Stedman, recalled his noble upbringing. His mother had put him out to four successive wet nurses, each one failing to handle him properly. One rolled over on top of him in her sleep, nearly suffocating him. Another dropped him so severely that he suffered lifelong periodic convulsions ever after. The third carted him beneath an old structure that collapsed, nearly killing him. Finally, he lamented, "the fourth proved to be a thief, and deprived me even of my very baby clothes."

Despite all of these shortcomings of the professional wet nurse, the convenience of her service allowed her to stay in business much longer than one would otherwise expect. As the 18th century drew to a close, however, many people, particularly Britons, had turned their backs on wet nurses. In 1781 it was happily reported that there had recently been a steady decline in childhood rickets (caused by specific nutritional deficiencies) due primarily to "more maternal attention to the suckling and rearing of children." A bit later, Mme. Roland found the nerve to demand that a clause be included in her marriage license granting her maternal nursing rights. Still, wet nurses remained in fairly general demand. In 1780, the Police Chief of Paris estimated that of 21,000 children being born each year in that city, only 700 were nursed by their mothers; another 700 were nursed at home by live-in nurses, and some 17,000 were still being sent to country wet nurses. (The rest were presumably nursed by relatives or friends.)

In the New World, some American colonists were apparently eager to carry on the old aristocratic tradition of using wet nurses. Samuel Sewall, a Massachusetts Colony merchant, almost boastfully informed people that "Joseph Brisco's wife gives my son suck." A Colonial newspaper in 1754 noted this: "If a woman knows her husband can spare three to six shillings per week, she . . . will persuade the good man to get a nurse, by pretending indisposition." Wet nursing never became widespread in the New World, however, partly because it was already being shunned by many of the more enlightened Britons, but also because there were too few people of substantial means to support any growth of the occupation.

Wet nursing was gradually transformed during the 19th century. Whereas once it had been thought a luxury for the rich, it was increasingly viewed as a necessity for the poor. The Industrial Revolution had led many peasant women into the factories of nearby towns and cities, where they labored from sunrise to sunset for meager wages. They had hardly any time for nursing chores, and wet nurses—sometimes professionals, sometimes relatives or friends—were needed. Obviously, these women could pay little, and the quality of nursing declined even further. The upper classes, at the same time, were more frustrated than ever before with the problems of putting-out their offspring to careless and often heartless mercenaries.

As the 20th century approached, traditional views of children were changing, too. Unlike the view of children as mere "property," beings "to be seen and not heard," new psychological insight was fostering the image of the infant as a human being, with rights and feelings. Advances in medicine and nutrition also made it apparent that many of the old ways of handling babies were unhealthy. The growing middle class came to prefer maternal nursing over "putting-out"; and those who could afford to do so made the extra effort to hire wet nurses strictly on a live-in basis.

Bottle feeding was more widely practiced by the 1830s after a *midwife*, Mme. Breton, marketed a new type of artificial nipples and bottles. Before this, a cow's or goat's teat was commonly cooked in limewater and used for the same purpose. In Russia, the *saska*, a mild poultice, was tied up in a long bag at which infants sucked—"often so effectually that they draw the saska down into the throat, and are suffocated." Bottles were safer than these poultices, and more convenient than nursing. In cities where women's rights had become a fashionable cause by the 1890's, bottle-feeding became the topic of the day. Still, contaminated and poorly preserved or poorly sterilized milk fed through a bottle was considered a major cause of infant mortality before pasteurization.

To solve this problem, a great many families decided to introduce babies to solid food much sooner than had been traditionally done. Despite the alleged and real health hazards of this practice, it became increasingly popular. Many a newborn was given a pacifier made of food that had been tied in a small bag. These children were virtually dependent on whole foods by the fifth or sixth week of their lives, despite warnings to delay the process until at least the sixth month.

Bottle-feeding and early food introduction con-tributed to the decline of wet nursing as an occupation, because mothers or their servants could tend to these chores themselves. In truth, wet nurses themselves were repeatedly exposed for using these very same conveniences—all the while accepting payment for wet nursing.

The wet nursing occupation generally declined first in the most industrialized parts of the world. England, America, and the major cities of the Continent. It remained quite common in the rural areas of France until the early 20th century, and in Germany and Italy right up to World War II; and it was a proud profession in Russia before the Revolution of 1917. The 19th-century rise of municipal hospitals and institutionalized childbirth created some jobs for wet nurses within those settings, but bottle-feeding had appeared at about the

A single nurse or nanny might have charge of several children in the nursery that became both her home and workplace. (From Harper's New Monthly Magazine)

same time, so these opportunities were short-lived. Bottle-feeding took a while to catch on in less industrialized countries. While it was the rage in Paris, a survey of St. Petersburg, Russia, in the 1870's showed that of some 8,000 children cared for at the Oldenburg Hospital for Children, only one-third were bottled-fed.

Modern bottle, milk, and baby food preparations and processing have made wet nursing a thing of the past in industrialized nations today, although it continues in many undeveloped parts of the world. In recent decades, maternal nursing has become popular again in many countries, but wet nursing has not revived along with it.

Meanwhile, other child-care occupations have arisen. The first of these was the British *nanny*, who emerged in the Victorian era. She was initially hired as a *mother's helper*, where wet nurses were no longer employed. Gentlewomen took in mother's helpers as domestic *companions* for their babies and children, but soon gave them much broader responsibilities. Separate "nurseries" were set up where the nanny and child lived and worked in virtual seclusion from the rest of the household. Nannies were given such total control over the infants that in some cases weeks or months could pass without either of the parents speaking to or even setting eyes upon their children. The nanny became a *tutor* as well as a second mother.

Many observers of the glorious Victorian era insisted that the nanny was the heart and soul of the British empire. In France and Germany, during this same time, only the general house servants cared for the children, having no special duties as did the British nanny.

While some well-to-do families still hire nannies, personal tutors, and servants for their children, *babysitters* (in Britain often called *child minders*), *nursery schools*, and *day-care centers* have become the most practical and popular child-care alternatives for the middle classes throughout most of the world. The private nursery of the fine Victorian town houses has inspired the growth of public nurseries or nursery schools in the 20th

Nannies often wore uniforms similar to those worn by house-maids, with cap and frilled apron. (Authors' archives, 1899)

century, as many more women have left the home for opportunities in the business world. Day care centers were created for the same purpose, but they typically keep children for longer hours and are often sponsored and operated by state or local governments. While *nursery school workers* were originally little more than child custodians, their roles have become increasingly complex since the 1960's, and they are usually more likely now to be trained and often licensed *teachers* as well as "sitters."

Babysitters are really a functional offshoot of domestic servants. They, too, have been used increasingly as women have joined the work force in rising numbers. At one time, they were typically employed mostly to cover leisure hours, while parents attended social functions. The babysitter, in such cases, acted purely as a custodian—sitting with the children, tending to their immediate needs, and putting them to sleep for the night.

Gradually, babysitters have been called on to act more like nannies, who care for children during the parents' work day for periods of weeks, months, or years. Babysitters usually come into the house to tend a child for as long as the parents are away, and then return to their own homes. Sometimes they are employed to live in; occasionally the child is brought to their home for care. Young girls are often hired for short hours of babysitting, but mature women—often mothers themselves, and in many cases recent immigrants—usually handle more regular and lengthy assignments. Babysitting, like nursery school and day-care teaching, is almost totally dominated by female workers.

In modern times, child nurses have often been drawn from among minority or immigrant groups. (National Archives, 42-SPB-18, Washington, D.C., c. 1910)

For related occupations in this volume, *Helpers and Aides*, see the following:
Servants and Other Domestic Laborers

For related occupations in other volumes of the series, see the following:

Healers (forthcoming):
 Midwives and Obstetricians

in *Manufacturers and Miners* (forthcoming):
 Factory Workers

in *Restaurateurs and Innkeepers* (forthcoming):
 Dairy Operators

in *Scholars and Priests* (forthcoming):
 Teachers

Drivers

Throughout history *drivers* have used vehicles or beasts of burden to transport people and goods. Unlike *movers* and *porters*, who have specialized in doing the actual hauling, drivers are primarily responsible for directing vehicles or handling animals. Closely related to drivers are *ferriers* and *boat operators*, who have used their craft on waterways.

Beasts of burden were domesticated early—the Arabian camel in about 1800 B.C., for example. At first animals were handled either by *herders*, who moved them seasonally, or by *merchants*, who used them to bear their goods. People were not employed specifically to drive carts. Once animals began to be used for pulling vehicles, merchants and *farmers* drove the carts themselves. Likewise, *charioteers* in the Near East, as well as in India and China, were more likely to be *soldiers* than professional drivers, though some charioteers in Rome acted as *racers*, vying for extravagant prizes in the popular chariot-racing events.

No sooner had chariots been invented than drivers were appointed to drive them for passengers like this Ethiopian princess under her umbrella. (From History of Egypt, *by Clara Erskine Clement, 1903)*

Ferriers, on the other hand, operated early. Permanent bridges across rivers were rare, because many rivers in Eurasia and Egypt tended to flood badly in the springtime. Besides, permanent bridges made a settlement vulnerable to an enemy's attack. People in these regions solved the problem of river-crossings by developing temporary boat-bridges—much like modern pontoon bridges—which could be destroyed quickly in case of invasion or taken apart in anticipation of spring floods. These were used right up into modern times, but only at major crossing points.

At other points, ferriers operated raft-like craft to take people across the water. Sometimes these ferriers were independent entrepreneurs who had been able to claim and hold on to a particularly valuable crossing point. At other times, such as in those periods when India had a strong central government, ferry operators were under the jurisdiction, if not in the employ, of the government itself, which appointed supervisors to see that the ferry service was operated in a manner fair to all.

Though ferry operators could sometimes take advantage of travelers forced to cross at the point they controlled, the advantage was not all theirs. Ferry operators in India were repeatedly warned over the centuries to be sure to get their fare before taking the party across—or risk not getting it at all.

In Europe, ferries were operated on the Rhine as early as 2000 B.C., for use by traders on the early Amber Route. The wrecks of many of these ferries have been found underwater by modern archaeologists.

Ferry operators were less needed in later times in the lands controlled by the Romans, with their penchant for building massive and permanent bridges, even over small streams. Julius Caesar once boasted that he marched an army from Rome to Iberia without getting their feet wet. But elsewhere, and after the decline of the Romans and their strong central government, ferry operators continued to operate in the old way until modern times.

On waterways like China's Imperial Canal, boats of all descriptions operated; craft were hauled upstream by trackers pulling from a towpath on shore. (From The New America and the Far East *by G. Waldo Browne, 1901)*

Boat operators also worked on suitable rivers throughout the Old World, again either as entrepreneurs or as government employees. They generally made use of the river currents in heading downstream. In the other direction, they had to use *trackers*, workers who hauled the boats along from the shore. This was an especially difficult chore in areas of rapids, such as on the Nile. In some cases special paths had to be cut out of rock cliffs for the trackers to walk on, as on China's Yangtze River. On rivers with slow-flowing currents, such as some in Mesopotamia in the dry season, boat operators could pole their boats upstream. The same was true in some canals, such as those that served as prime waterways for transporting bulk items in China from at least 2,000 years ago.

Aside from seasonal variations in the water level, boat operators, whether hauling goods or passengers, faced another hazard on the rivers: They shared the waterways with *river pirates*. Pirates on rivers like the Tigris, the Euphrates, and the Danube were infamous. There was sufficient traffic over the centuries for them to continue making a living. Because of these pirates, boat operators were never very numerous until modern times, and then only when strong central government provided soldiers or police to free rivers from pirates. Land routes were more heavily used instead.

Professional drivers, as distinct from those handling animals or vehicles in connection with other occupations, began to emerge in the East with the rise of trade. At around the beginning of the Christian era—with Rome in the West, the Han Dynasty in China, and powerful civilizations in India and Central Asia—trade flourished. The caravans that snaked across Asia traversed great distances over widely varied terrain. No pack animal could bear its load over the full 5,000-mile distance, nor were all animals equally suited to different climes. As a result, merchants accompanying their goods across Asia generally had to exchange animals several times, using camels in desert regions, mules or yaks in mountains, and horses on the high steppes, for example, and often using more than one group of each.

A group of *animal handlers* developed, who specialized in raising and training animals for caravans, bringing exhausted animals back into working condition, and supplying fresh beasts to traders. Often these handlers would accompany the merchant trains to handle the animals themselves, working as *camel drivers*, *hostlers* (persons who handle horses), or *muleteers*. Later, in Islamic times, camel drivers were extremely important on the pilgrimages to Mecca. They supplied and took care of camels for the pilgrims to use in crossing the deserts, from western Asia and northern Africa to Arabia. Camel drivers were equally important in the gold-for-salt trade across the Sahara between northern Africa and cities like Timbuktu in the old Sudan.

In Europe, drivers did not become clearly distinguished as professionals until the revival of commerce that accompanied the region's cultural Renaissance. The Age of Discovery introduced changes that made

On caravan journeys, drivers were responsible for training, feeding, and handling the camels or other animals. (From History of Egypt, by Clara Erskine Clement, 1903)

products from the East more available to a broader range of potential European consumers. Water routes were discovered that directly connected the East to the Renaissance merchants of the Mediterranean world. These new routes largely bypassed the Arab and Indian middlemen. As shipbuilding and navigation techniques improved, a great East-West trade was opened up, and many more reasonably priced goods were made available to relatively large numbers of purchasers. As the trade in these goods expanded north of the Italian ports, roads were improved, bridges built, and more uniform transport laws instituted.

It was in this atmosphere of long-haul merchandising that it first became desirable to employ professional *carters* to deliver goods to distant markets. At first these people traveled on foot, carrying packs on their backs. Later they pushed or pulled small-wheeled carts, and in time mules were hitched to the carts instead to make the job still faster and easier.

At the beginning of the Commercial Revolution, in the 16th century, most merchants sold their wares near the ports where their ships came in. Those who wanted to reach other customers generally undertook the transport of goods on their own, not trusting common *carriers* to handle their monies and merchandise. With the growth of commerce, though, trade expanded so greatly, and the markets for imported goods became so vast, that merchants could not possibly handle the direct delivery of such items any longer. Their energies were better spent in making arrangements for purchases and sales, and in expanding their markets to the furthest reaches of Western Europe.

At about the same time, other developments occured that made the employment of drivers to make deliveries more attractive and practical. Banks began issuing paper notes and letters of credit to be used instead of bulky gold and silver. Since such notes were redeemable only to authorized parties, the likelihood of robbery—either from the *highwaymen* who incessantly harassed travelers and *messengers*, or from the carriers themselves—was seriously reduced. Also, wagons and carriages were being built in the 16th century that had the capacity to handle larger and heavier loads than had ever before been possible.

Horses were soon being used to pull these heavy loads. Horses had been used primarily for combat in Europe before the 12th century A.D. But after that time, they were increasingly transformed into beasts of burden for agricultural enterprises. As crop yields rose to unprecedented heights, many of these horses were hitched to wagons for the transport of produce. By the 16th century they had largely replaced both mules and oxen as the chief haulers of the heavy carriages and wagons being built to meet new transport demands. Horses proved to be swifter and stronger than other animals, and so became the chief source of power for vehicles, carts, and carriages right up to the 20th century.

The *stage wagon* of the 16th century was a massive vehicle pulled by a 10-horse team. Used essentially for heavy cargo transport, it was rarely driven, but rather was guided by a *teamster*, who walked ahead of the team, pulling on the lead horse. In both France and Britain, *stagecoaches* appeared at about the same time. They provided a means of human transportation, essentially for aristocrats and gentlefolk. They were usually driven by private *coachmen*, who also served as domestic *servants* and *stablemen* when they were not driving. The first professional drivers of public transport vehicles were those who operated the popular *hackney carriages* beginning as early as the 16th century. These were mostly for people of ample means seeking short-distance rides in and about a few large cities such as London and Paris. By 1650 there were some 300 hackney carriages in England, the majority of them being privately and independently owned and driven.

Old gun-carriages, in use since the 15th century, inspired the design for the multi-passenger stagecoach that carried persons between towns or on even longer

At post stations all along stage routes, grooms and hostlers un-hitched exhausted teams and hitched up fresh ones—here, on the great Siberian road. (*From* The Century Illustrated Monthly Magazine)

rides. In Italy public *coachmen* driving coaches known as *vetturini*, catered to a finer clientele and even began including windows for their passengers' pleasure. Also for the more elegant passenger, sedan chairs could be hired in Europe between the 16th and 18th centuries. They had long been used in China. Typically, the sedan chair was a throne-like seat affixed to parallel poles; it was initially carried by as many as eight *bearers* in China, but usually only two in Europe. The *roulette*, a sedan-cart similar to an Asian *rickshaw*, was mounted on two wheels and was drawn by only one man. An especially popular vehicle, the roulette was sometimes privately owned and driven by a servant, but was more frequently driven for hire up and down city streets by private driver-operators. Even wheelbarrows with sails were pushed or driven in China for public transportation.

The *cabriolet*, or *cab*, offered quick cross-town transportation for middle-class people. The earliest *cab drivers* could accommodate no more than two passengers in their two-wheeled, one-horse, covered vehicles. By the late 18th century there were some 2,000 cabs competing for business in Paris alone. By that time, though, their operation had become so careless, the drivers so coarse, and the roads so rutty that even the middle classes were reluctant to avail themselves of such convenience. In the early 19th century, *Turkish cabs* or *arabas* were commonly found in Eastern Europe. They were powered by oxen for regular passengers, horses for aristocrats. Mules were used by Spanish cab drivers, who stationed themselves at difficult mountain passes to transport carriage passengers and cargo in several shuttles, until the rugged terrain had been crossed.

Municipalities became involved in the transportation business right from the start, although in a fairly limited capacity. City *bus drivers* were hired in Paris as early as the 17th century to operate horse-drawn buses. By the 1660's, the city had a small fleet of these eight-seaters that ran a regular town schedule, as posted, for a single flat rate.

In the same period, as cities expanded, drivers and passengers increasingly used the waterways that ran through many cities. These were often far more comfortable than streets and roads, which were pitted and often muddy. The most skillful *watermen* were, of course, the *gondoliers* of Venice, where canals themselves were the "city streets." But watermen operated in many major cities. Sometimes they operated simply like ferriers, transporting people across rivers or lakes where no bridges existed. But often they used the water as a highway, transporting people along rivers to various parts of the city. Their craft—and the watermen themselves—varied with the clientele and the area they served. The graceful Venetian gondolas serving prosperous passengers were richly furnished and cushioned; the same was true on some northern rivers, such as the portions of the Thames above London, where the rich and powerful often had their private estates.

Of all the boat operators on inland canals and waterways, Venice's gondoliers are the most famous. (From Men: A Pictorial Archive From Nineteenth-Century Sources, *by Jim Harter, Dover, 1980)*

Watermen who served the poorer, rougher, working sections of the cities were often untrustworthy. While some were surely hardworking sorts, many had a well-deserved bad reputation, having "no settled place of abode and [being] idle and profligate persons," according to one 18th-century report. Young boys apprenticed to them were often ill-treated, being starved and beaten, and sometimes were not taught a trade—one young

Today's modern taxi drivers, fire-fighters, and police officers might well feel that modern technology had brought little progress in traffic congestion. (By Gustave Doré, from London: A Pilgrimage, *1872)*

apprentice found that his "master" did not even own a boat. Worse than that, many young apprentices were taken on by watermen, who then arranged to have the boys taken into the navy, the wages and prize-money the boys earned all going into the pockets of the masters. It was in an attempt to cure such abuses that many watermen, notably in London, were licensed by the municipality, and required to carry with them the label or ticket that was proof of their licensing. Watermen gradually lost some of their bad reputation, if only by assisting *firefighters* in doing their vital work in the fire-prone cities. Indeed, the firefighters' uniform, down to the licensing label, was—in England, at least—modeled after the uniform of the watermen.

The period just before the Industrial Revolution saw a great rise in public transportation, but an even greater one in cargo transport. *Wagoners* and *cart* or *carriage drivers* had become indispensable to the inland transport of goods that was making Europe the leading economic force in the world. Yet, during this same period, the early drivers, who had owned and operated their own vehicles, virtually disappeared. They were replaced instead by large enterprises that owned sizable fleets of vehicles. To operate these vehicles, the owners hired and dispatched, according to fixed schedules, professional drivers, coachmen, and wagoners.

Transportation was an expensive undertaking during the early modern era. Driver-transporters could own independent businesses only as long as they could compete with the speed of large horse-drawn wagons for cargo or comfortable carriages for passengers. Both were extremely expensive to purchase, maintain, and operate, however. Only grubby little cabs or small-time country carts were cheap enough for a person of average means to both own and drive.

Capital took on considerable importance in the profession from early on. *Innkeepers* became the most common operators of transport firms. They were already located at strategic travel junctions. Besides, they often owned or operated coaches and wagons to serve their own business anyway. Inns had stalls to keep horses, and barns and courtyards for carriages and carts. They also had an ample supply of driving and porterage labor drawn from the hangers-on who resided on the premises or frequented the attached alehouses. In addition to all that, innkeepers often had decent capital resources or at least potential credit opportunities. Many became public *transport contractors*, operating passenger coach services in addition to wagon freight-hauling concerns.

The drivers themselves were a scraggly crew. Sometimes they were off-season peasants, who had just finished reaping their grape or grain harvests and were in search of short-term employment. They would drive produce wagons from rural to urban areas, or cabs in the large cities. Some of them even worked independently with their own cabs or carts, but they were few and far between, because of the considerable expense of inland travel. Most of the carriers, carters, coachmen, and wagoners were drawn from the local mob of roughs and toughs who made drivers notorious for their rude speech and rough manners. At many a transport

Though noted for their speed, stagecoach drivers in early modern Europe often spent enormous amounts of time inching out of mud or up hills. (From Die kleinen Leiden des menschlichen Lebens, *by Jean Grandeville)*

headquarters—which inns certainly were—off-duty drivers were the worst enemy of passengers wishing to protect their baggage and valuables.

One observer noted in 1768 that "Our stagecoachmen are perpetually drinking, they no sooner descry a sign than they find themselves thirsty." The *London Guide* noted in 1818 that "most people come up to town by coaches and waggons . . ." and that "the inns at which . . . [they] put up are places of special resort for thieves and cheats of a better sort." A good many of this "better sort" were wage-earning drivers.

The situation eventually became so bad in London that police were hired to patrol inn yards. By 1832 the increased speed of stagecoaches seems to have resulted in the hiring of more sober and responsible drivers. The London *Quarterly Review* of 1832 includes a report that "a coachman drunk on his box is now a rarity—a coachman quite sober, was even within our memory, still more so."

By the late 18th and early 19th centuries, many transportation companies were combining freight and passenger services for long hauls. In the United States, John Palmer opened a stagecoach line headquartered in Bath, Maine, which required drivers to be responsible for both passengers and the mails as early as 1784. Having wooed the government postal agency with promises of speedy delivery, frequent horse changes, and sober, honest, responsible drivers, Palmer became one of the first private persons to procure a post office contract for mail transport.

The American push westward soon paved the way for many stagecoach operators to send their drivers into territories where postal and freight services found it difficult to venture, bearing passengers, official mails, and other cargo. Coaches were made bigger and more comfortable, sometimes seating up to 14 passengers. The more regular, highly traveled lines featured coaches pulled by horses; but many less significant ones, which rattled up mountainsides and through quiet little towns and valleys, had coaches pulled by mules, goats, or even large dogs. Drivers were obliged to have a definite command of a wide variety of animals.

The American West provided some of the most colorful characters in the history of the driving vocation. Muleteers, teamsters, and ox-cart drivers were common, later to be replaced by rakish stagecoach drivers, celebrated for their bravery, skill, and stamina. Covered wagons traveled west together in caravans called wagon trains. These were led by *wagon-masters*, who were responsible not so much for driving as for safely guiding travelers and pioneers through deserts and hostile territories to their destinations. Passenger-coach and mail-coach drivers also faced treacherous driving conditions and threats from both Native Americans and bands of *robbers*. Most of these robbers were men, but persistent rumors had it that some were women, fleeing ultra-polite Victorian society, and choosing instead the freedom of being outlaws. Perhaps the most adventurous of all frontier drivers were those on the express coaches that made deliveries of gold, silver, currency, and other valuables to and from mines and banks. These men were pioneers in the armored-car services that would blossom in the 20th century.

Wells Fargo and Company, organized in 1852 during the great California Gold Rush, was probably the greatest of these carriers, and it eventually bought out the famous but short-lived Pony Express. The company was originally a banking operation, but its owners soon found that the need for safely shipping money, valuables, bullion, and packages was so considerable in this lawless region, that the expansion of this aspect of their business would be most profitable. Possessing the most extensive stagecoach network in the United States in the 19th century, Wells Fargo delivered packages as part of its express business until the United States Post Office began its parcel post services in 1912.

Stagecoach lines in Europe and America considerably improved transportation for passengers. As travel and long-distance commerce continued to increase, toll roads were built in many countries, often as private enterprises. *Tollhouse tenders* or *tollgate keepers*—predecessors of those who staff the toll booths on modern expressways and bridges—were assigned to collect tolls from travelers passing through. These employees were often subject to great harassment, especially when the roads were in ill repair, and people sometimes "ran the gates" without paying the required toll.

In the 18th century overland transport was still enormously expensive and costly for bulk goods. As a result, the late 18th and early 19th centuries saw an explosion of canal-building. Sparked by England, the movement quickly spread to mainland Europe and North America, as channels were cut through or around rapids to make rivers navigable, as on the St. Lawrence River, and canals were dug to join navigable bodies of water. Some of these were water-level cuts—the largest and best-known being the Suez Canal—while others used a series of locks, as does the Panama Canal, to carry craft from one level to another. In Europe and North America canals large and small were built carrying both agricultural products and goods from emerging industries throughout the land.

The result was that a whole subculture grew up on the rivers. Whole families lived on canal boats, transporting goods and, increasingly, passengers. In this they were independently evolving a pattern that had long existed in China, where canals had been a vital part of the transportation system for many centuries. Beasts of burden, like the old mule named Sal on the Erie Canal, were used to haul barges along, and many people along the canals made their living tending the animals. Other workers tended the locks, handling the gates and controlling the flow of water that brought barges and canal boats from one level to the next in their cross-country journey.

Canal folk were a breed apart. Many townfolk looked longingly at their life, free of the social restrictions of settled villages. What they did not see were the hardships. The constant damp, often combined with cold, was one of the hardships—a problem facing all those who make their life on the water.

The development of steamboats added a new dimension to inland shipping, making canals and rivers busier than ever—and making the steamboat captain, *pilot*, and crew romantic figures as well, as witness the writings of Mark Twain (Samuel Clemens) in *Life on the Mississippi*.

Technology also increasingly affected the canals. Massive machinery came to be used to handle the locks, and *lock tenders* became more like engineers. Ferries, too, acquired motors, and small rafts were often replaced by engine-driven craft.

But the Industrial Revolution of the 19th and 20th centuries moved so fast that new forms of transportation soon moved to the fore. Railroads and, finally, electric and gasoline engines completely broke people's dependence on animal power for transportation. Drivers were no longer all-purpose animal handlers, but gradually became specialists in running one or another type of machine for transportation.

Change came slowly at first, as can be expected, since many drivers of horse-pulled vehicles feared the new technology. Steam buses and coaches both met with relative technological success during their trials in London and Paris. Goldsworthy Gurney had established a regular steam coach service in England as early as 1831, and Walter Hancock's in London at about the same time was so successful that at one time it was carrying up to 30 passengers per run.

Horse-led coach operators did not appreciate the competition, however, and drivers did not want to learn to operate the new vehicles. Pressure from these special interest groups resulted in the passing of the Red Flag law in England. According to this statute, steam coaches went so fast and were so dangerous and disruptive that they had to be preceded by a *footman* waving a red flag to warn people away. The steam coaches were slowed down in all the confusion, extra personnel had to be hired to comply with the law, and the public lost confidence in this form of transportation. Steam coaches had been effectively driven out of business by the 1840's, but the law remained intact until 1896 when automobiles made their appearance.

In the non-industrialized areas of the world, of course, drivers continued to operate animal-powered rigs, as they still do today. The *peónes* of South and Central America were employed in the driving of oxen or mule-pulled *carro de boi*, a sort of chunky cart with solid wooden wheels. But in the newly industrialized world, drivers would soon be operating—almost exclusively—engine-powered rigs.

Trains took over a great deal of the transportation needs in the modern nations during the 19th century. Steamboats, paddle steamers, riverboats, ferries, and water-cabs competed with the railroads for a while, but by the end of the century the railroad clearly reigned supreme. *Locomotive engineers* became one of the most important types of drivers in the newly in-

While this railroad engineer had adopted casual, jaunty dress, his coworker, the conductor, wore a more formal uniform. (After H. Alken, 1852)

dustrialized world. In the great age of the railroads, engineers had top status, heading many a child's list of "What I Want to Be When I Grow Up." Not far behind were the *brakemen*, the *firemen* who stoked the engine, and the *conductors*, who took the tickets and supervised the passenger and baggage cars. To watchful eyes, their jobs had both the glamor of traveling far distances to new, wide-open lands and the excitement of new technology.

Trains carried heavy metals and raw materials to the factories where they were needed for production processes. They delivered food from the country and manufactured goods from the factory to the vastly enlarged cities, where consumers depended on prompt service. And they took passengers across mountains, deserts, and prairies. Trains remained the chief means of freight transport until after World War II. Early mine railroads in Paris, New York, and London were opened as subways to handle intra-city passenger traffic, beginning with the famous Thames Tunnel in 1843. The most popular form of intra-city transit by the beginning of the 20th century was the electric street-car or trolley car.

But soon automobiles, trucks, and motor buses made their appearance. The first regular motor bus service in the United States was established in New York in 1905. In the years after World War I, the small delivery truck became an increasingly common sight in most towns and cities. Its drivers were responsible for regular deliveries, as well as route sales, by which they not only serviced customers but also tried to persuade them to buy additional merchandise. Trucks became ever more important after World War II, as tractor-trailers increasingly replaced trains for long-distance transport. In the United States *truckers*, or *truck drivers*, were organized by the Team Drivers International and the Teamsters National unions in 1905. The Teamsters Union, still a very powerful and cohesive force among truck drivers in the United States, undertook the organization of long-distance truck drivers in 1933.

Though they got little public attention, workers in the railroad's signal box, here at London Bridge station, kept trains running smoothly. (From Illustrated London News)

Drivers of mechanized vehicles are very different from traditional drivers, yet they have retained many historical ties to their predecessors. Mass and rapid transit have placed greater emphasis than ever before on speed and promptness. The complexity of traffic systems and the sophistication of the vehicles being driven often require drivers who are not only sober and attentive, but who also have received some training. Bus drivers for large transportation companies must often undergo several years of training, but school-bus drivers have notoriously been undertrained. Cab drivers sometimes undergo training, but it is seldom very substantial, relating more to local geography than to driving. Railroad engineers and long-haul truckers are highly trained, while route delivery drivers are rarely trained.

Even into the late 20th century, horse-drawn carts, carriages, buses, and cabs are still seen. But today only a few luxury horse-drawn carriages carry nostalgic passengers around large cities; their drivers are customarily attired in Victorian-styled costume, in keeping with the most memorable era of the tradition.

Armored car services to banks and other cash-rich institutions have become increasingly important in the modern world. Armored car drivers have extremely dangerous jobs. To compete with Wells Fargo, Brinks developed a fleet of armored coaches, beginning with its 1891 contract with Western Electric to deliver its payroll. Brinks' drivers became the target of many ambushes in the mid-20th century, after two of its drivers were killed by robbers in 1917. Many others have been killed and wounded in the line of duty since then. Most recently, armored-car drivers in Europe and North America have

In these early motorized vehicles called charabancs, *neither driver nor passengers had protection from the elements. (Library of Congress, 1904)*

been targeted by terrorists, who hold them up and frequently kill or maim them, going after funds for their underground activities.

Drivers of all sorts work in today's world. Truck drivers are sometimes thought of as rugged, unrefined individuals, much like the public coachmen of bygone ages, while private drivers, called *chauffeurs*, have a spiffy, tailored image much like that of one-time domestic or private coachmen. Cab drivers rush and scurry, just as the horse-cab drivers once did, eagerly seeking to outdo the competition in quickness and aggressiveness. While most drivers work for large transportation firms, many others work for municipalities; some even operate independently, owning their vehicles. In most industrialized countries, the vehicles themselves are generally bought new and kept in quite good repair. But in poorer parts of the world, vehicles 20 or even 30 years old, many of them cast-offs from private uses, are pressed into service and often grossly overloaded, carrying twice the number of passengers or amount of goods the vehicle was intended to bear.

Whatever their sophistication, training, or professional levels, drivers provide services that have never been more needed. Today's world revolves around transportation. Trucks carry food and manufactured items to a great mass of consumers, who would otherwise be at a loss to obtain most of these items. While a great many people now drive their own private automobiles to work and on errands, mass transit has always been important to city-dwellers. It is also vital to the swelling ranks of suburbanites, who must seek alternatives to serious traffic congestion, rising gasoline prices, and threatened oil shortages. Society seems now to be held together by a network of highways and rails, delivery routes and transit schedules. Without the services, skills, and perseverance of drivers, the aptly named arteries of this network would deteriorate, and the lifeblood of the culture and economy to which we have become accustomed would cease to flow.

For related occupations in this volume, *Helpers and Aides*, see the following:
Firefighters
Movers
Private Guards and Detectives
Servants and Other Domestic Laborers

For related occupations in other volumes of the series, see the following:
in *Builders*:
Architects and Contractors
Roadbuilders
in *Communicators*:
Messengers and Couriers
in *Financiers and Traders*:
Bankers and Financiers
Merchants and Shopkeepers
in *Harvesters*:
Farmers
in *Performers and Players* (forthcoming):
Athletes
Racers
in *Restaurateurs and Innkeepers* (forthcoming):
Innkeepers
in *Scientists and Technologists* (forthcoming):
Engineers
in *Warriors and Adventurers* (forthcoming):
Robbers and Other Criminals
Sailors
Soldiers

Exterminators and Pest Controllers

Although insects and many kinds of animals have been worrisome pests since ancient times, they were virtually impossible to control at all until the discovery of pesticides in the late 19th and early 20th centuries. *Priests* and *magicians* would try to ward off crop-killing blights with prayers, rites and chants. But the only truly professional *pest controllers* before the 19th century A.D. were the *rat* and *dog catchers*. Rat catchers have the longer history of the two, dating back certainly to medieval times, and probably even earlier. People knew little of the role that insects and rats played in disease before the 19th century. Rats were controlled essentially as nuisances and because they ate into food stores. Local farmers or peasants would sometimes rent out their pet cats or weasels for use in catching rats, and royal and noble householders sometimes appointed official rat catchers.

The increased use of water travel and long voyages in the 16th century and thereafter created opportunities for rat catchers. They were employed to try to save precious stores of food, without which the passengers and crew could well starve to death. Still, without proper methods of food preservation, food spoiled and became virtually worthless anyway. Often, sailors were so starved for something "fresh" that they paid shipboard rat catchers rather handsomely for live or recently killed rats.

The growth of cities after the 16th century led to the creation of publicly funded positions for municipal rat catchers and dog catchers. Dog catchers pursued stray dogs that could become public nuisances and sometimes dangerous. Many of these animal catchers sold off some of their catches to *butchers*, who were known to openly advertise and display their stock of freshly killed dogs, cats, and rats as late as the mid-19th century, even in such fine cities as Paris. During times of war and famine, this practice was especially common.

In the 20th century the relationship between animal pests and disease became clearly established. In 1900, for

Rat catchers often used poisons, dogs, and assistants to help them kill the rodents, which they then displayed as advertisements. (By Cornelis Visscher, 1655)

instance, Walter Reed discovered that yellow fever in the Panama Canal region was being carried and spread by infectious mosquitoes. Working with sanitation expert W. C. Gorgas, Reed established a massive clean-up and public health project, and the disease was arrested. Before then the large-scale canal, road, and rail construction projects of the 19th century had resulted in countless deaths and illnesses of workers exposed to the merciless onslaughts of such pests.

In modern times, public health education and sanitation have been important in reducing the likelihood of diseases caused by pests. Rat catchers largely became a thing of the past, as people developed increasingly efficient systems for picking up refuse and garbage and depositing it outside populated areas. Dog catchers continue to be employed by many municipalities, but they are frequently the butts of jokes, accused—often rightly—of being paid for doing little or nothing.

The use of pesticides, especially since World War II, has become the major factor in controlling pests. Farms where foods and grains are grown are now sprayed regularly with these chemicals to ward off insect infestations. (In addition, animals used for slaughter or dairying are treated with large doses of antibiotics to prevent the spread of pest-related illnesses as well as other diseases.)

On a smaller scale, householders can now buy a wide variety of pesticides and rat poisons to control pests on their own. But they may also employ *exterminators* who have the special training and expertise in the field to do so for them. Large institutions, especially those where foods are prepared and sold, generally employ licensed exterminators.

Of course, in these cases, the large chemical companies are now the real pest controllers, if only indirectly. Their products, while convenient and effective in the short term, have been widely condemned as being cumulatively poisonous to people through direct consumption of foods treated with them, and indirectly through wide-

ranging destruction to the environment. The problem of pest control is a serious and considerable one today. While higher agricultural yields may be of immediate benefit, the long-term damage to water supplies, and to forest and soil resources, poses a significant hazard, as does the inhalation and ingestion of these poisons. The problem is made worse because insects and other pests tend to develop a resistance to products used against them, so the products no longer work as well, if at all.

For related occupations in this volume, *Helpers and Aides*, see the following:
Sanitation Workers
For related occupations in other volumes of the series, see the following:
in *Builders*:
Construction Laborers
in *Restaurateurs and Innkeepers* (forthcoming):
Butchers
in *Scholars and Priests* (forthcoming):
Priests
in *Scientists and Technologists* (forthcoming):
Chemists
in *Warriors and Adventurers* (forthcoming):
Sailors

Firefighters

Firefighting as a profession is known only among the industrial countries and did not become common until the 19th century. The Egyptians mention fighting fires as early as the second century B.C., but no one took this on as a special responsibility. That did not happen until modern times and the growth of giant cities. Before that, fires were put out if the surrounding crowd could form a bucket brigade. That took no special equipment or training; people simply stood in line, passing buckets from a well to the fire. All it needed was enough level heads, and most neighborhoods had a few.

In 1666, London, then the largest city in the world, nearly burned to the ground. The city had grown tremendously in the previous 100 years. Buildings—most of wood—had been almost piled on top of one another, and they made for a fire hazard too big for any emergency group of citizens. The London insurance companies did not want their money burned up in paying benefits. To prevent another disaster, they called together the first professional teams for fighting fires, a practice that companies in other cities soon found useful. Even in America, with no city that could match a European capital, Benjamin Franklin founded Philadelphia's Union Fire Company in 1736.

But volunteer companies still did at least as much firefighting as the professionals. The volunteer companies often drew members from the upper classes;

Early firefighters were often hired by insurance companies, as signified by this one's badge, and their uniform was adapted from that of the waterman. (By W. H. Pyne, Costume of Great Britain, *1808)*

two Roosevelts served with one of New York City's early teams, for example. It was considered noble work; city people were grateful for protection. *Firefighters* showed up in popular songs, and stories circulated about the different brigades. Many earned nicknames, such as the "Red Heads."

The equipment was still simple. New York City installed its first engine, shipped from London, in 1731. Crowds gathered for the ceremony. The engine was trundled along on wooden wheels and had to be lifted up to take a corner. A fire brigade was still usually just a bucket line with accessories. Firefighters passed buckets into an engine's tub, from which the hoses were hand-pumped with water.

In the 19th century, the equipment improved, and the brigades became more tightly organized. The cities kept growing faster, and firefighting somehow had to keep pace. By the 1890's, the typical big city fire brigade

The danger and daring in firefighters' activities have always attracted public attention. (Advertising woodcut for The Poor of New York, *New York, 1857)*

worked at a high level of sophistication. Once an alarm bell went off, the stable doors swung open automatically and the horses would trot on their own to the engines. The typical company was divided into two teams: 12 men (including a foreman and an assistant) for the hose, and a handful to look after the engine. The engine, meant to provide steam power for the hoses, was started by a boiler in the fire station's basement. Once going, it was un-hooked, and the engine would head down the street trailing smoke.

A team of firefighters would then use several tons of equipment: life nets, lines to secure the hoses, possibly a battering ram, and always a variety of axes. A hook-and-ladder team carried all this, showing up at every fire. The new size of buildings made the ladders necessary. Even if a fire was in the basement, the firefighters preferred to get at it through a building's upper stories, working down carefully instead of heading straight into the blaze.

Some old practices made for spotty protection. New York City's "Red Heads," for example, would work only at night, a custom that lasted until 1870. The independent brigades could become rather quarrelsome, and at every fire there was a struggle for leadership. The custom called "first water" gave command to the company that got to a hydrant first. This system could not last long.

The solution to this problem was the creation of a united firefighting force. Napoleon had led the way with a municipal force for Paris at the start of the 19th century. But his example was not widely followed at first. Government fire departments spread widely only in the second half of the century. Through the next 50 years or so after that, city and private brigades overlapped. As late as the 1890's, any large American city had a Protective Patrol, Salvage Corps, or Fire Patrol paid for and staffed by the insurance companies. But the cities, now mammoth, needed their own municipal forces big enough to match those of the insurance companies. This meant coordinat-

The last run of this horse team marked the end of an era in Washington, D.C., as motorized fire trucks took over. (Library of Congress, 1925)

ing the brigades, so that even the private forces found their independence giving way. As early as 1867, the New York State legislature chartered the private fire brigades, organizing them under a Board of Fire Underwriters and a Fire Patrol Superintendent.

Through the 20th century, almost every industrial nation has organized its fire department in a military-like chain of command. In the United States, this works with the Fire Chief on top and Deputy Chiefs looking after their assigned districts. Each district is divided into three battalions, which are each in turn divided into approximately seven companies. The companies are organized around equipment, most being engine companies (for pumping water), and after that hook-and-ladder companies. As a matter of routine, a city fire alarm is answered by at least an engine company, a ladder company, and a rescue squad.

A company is headed by a captain and several lieutenants; there are usually three or four officers and anywhere from 15 to 30 regular firefighters. The captain acts like an officer in battle, sizing up the situation and deciding on tactics. The firefighters cannot argue with the captain's commands. They are trained to handle very precise jobs, each using a particular piece of equipment and, without orders, doing nothing else. No chance of confusion is allowed in the face of the fire.

Every country with firefighters sets up programs to train them, mixing in-class lessons with drills and on-the-job training. Most United States programs last eight weeks, finishing with a written test and, in some departments, a physical one as well. There has been considerable argument about the physical requirements, and several departments have been sued for allegedly using their standards to keep out women, who have often had difficulty entering the field. The tests are followed by a probation period that can last up to a year; during this time, recruits serve in a fire station while earning full status. Even when full-fledged, they may return to class to study for promotion or to learn about new equipment and techniques. Some fire departments have also begun three-to-four-year apprenticeship programs, an idea that seems to be catching on.

A city's fire department follows the same rules for promotion that the rest of a city's civil service does. Factors taken into account include superiors' reports, standard tests, and length of time on the job. There are always more applicants than a department has openings. Pensions are good, as much as 50 percent of salary after 20 to 25 years of service. Starting pay in the United States in these years averages $14,000 a year; the highest salaries range from $16,400 to $20,500 a year. Balanced against these salaries are the considerable physical hazards faced by all firefighters, not simply the direct hazards posed by the fire itself, but also the increasing exposure to dangerous chemicals, both in industrial fires and in home blazes, where synthetic materials can give off toxic fumes.

For related occupations in this volume, *Helpers and Aides*, see the following:
   Drivers
   Movers

For related occupations in other volumes of the series, see the following:
in *Financiers and Traders*:
   Insurers
in *Leaders and Lawyers*:
   Police Officers

Launderers

The work of cleaning, pressing, and folding clothes or other fabrics has traditionally been women's work, particularly housewives'. Throughout history, most people's laundry has been washed by the women in their own family. Slaves did laundry cleaning for wealthy households in ancient societies. Perhaps the earliest professionals in the field were the Roman *fullers*, who cleaned raw wool, treading it into mats with their feet in large wooden vats, drying it, and *fulling* it by fluffing it out. Many fullers got severe skin diseases from the harsh chemical solutions that they worked in for hours at a time. Fullers were generally men.

Beginning with the early modern era, the housework that had been done by slaves in earlier centuries was being turned over more and more to domestic servants.

The *laundress* was usually one of the lowest orders of servants, those who were left with the most unpleasant of all household chores. Only the wealthiest, fully staffed households retained a laundress, of course; other affluent families left the laundry to the *scullery maid* or, more commonly, to the single maid who handled all of the cleaning for the family. Some householders sent the laundry out to the cottage of a peasant woman, often a former servant who—now being married—took work in whenever she could. Many fine country estates had separate wash-houses where laundresses labored long hours washing, starching, pleating, and matting clothing, giving special care to frilly lace and petticoats.

In the days before there was adequate sewage disposal, town-house laundresses added significantly to the stench and sludge of the cities by dumping their buckets of dirty water into the middle of the narrow streets. It was hard enough carting heavy buckets of water from the well to the house to wash the clothes; few laundresses even thought of carting the used water to a less offensive

Launderers, often women, had a heavy job in washing clothes in tubs or streams, hanging them to dry, folding them, and often ironing them. (By W. H. Pyne, from Picturesque Views of Rural Occupations in Early Nineteenth-Century England)

Launderers often doubled as dyers, washing materials in large vats and turning them to see that they were evenly cleaned and then dyed. (From Diderot's Encyclopedia, *late 18th century)*

dumping spot. The streets of London in the 19th century were filled with laundry-women sitting on stools with their tubs before them on benches just outside the front doors of their residences. After the clothes were washed and buckets dumped, the clothes were usually carted to an upstairs bedroom, where they were hung out the window or on crude clotheslines.

Of course, before the 20th century, most people had many fewer clothes and a much greater tolerance for dirt and wrinkles, so there was somewhat less laundry to do. Ironing had commonly been tended to by household laundresses as early as the 15th century. Fullers—active in both medieval and modern cities—used chemicals and special solutions (which they promptly dumped in nearby rivers) to remove spots and stains from fabrics. Cloth was very expensive, and many people preferred sending clothes and other fabrics out to the fuller for sprucing up or to the *clothesmender* for repair than to engage the *tailor* to make new clothes, drapes, and the like.

In the 20th century, household washing machines have replaced laundresses and—except in the larger cities—only fine fabrics are generally sent out to be chemically "dry-cleaned." Even so, commercial launderers did a fairly decent business of washing and pressing fine shirts and dresses until recent decades, when synthetic and permanent-press fabrics became widely marketed. Many small dry-cleaning establishments now specialize in the treatment of hard-to-handle materials such as furs and leathers. Many such establishments also do small repairs on leather goods like shoes and purses, as well as sewing, hemming, and reweaving. To some extent, then, they have taken on the chores of the fuller and the clothesmender of old.

Large commercial laundries have been important since the early 20th century. They deal particularly in large commercial accounts—hotels, restaurants, dormitories. Some large institutions, such as hospitals, run their own on-site laundry services. Diaper-services regularly distribute and clean diapers, although the recent widespread use of disposable diapers has cut into this business. Most *laundry workers* in large establishments are women, working for menial wages in a factory-like environment of large machines and conveyor belts.

One of the most recent developments in this field is the growth of laundromats or self-service laundry establishments. The operators of these businesses provide coin-operated washing and drying machines for those who have no access to them otherwise. Customers at these places generally do their own laundry, while the operators maintain the premises and the machines.

For related occupations in this volume, *Helpers and Aides*, see the following:
Servants and Other Domestic Laborers

For related occupations in other volumes of the series, see the following:
in *Clothiers*:
Dyers and Other Cloth Finishers
Tailors and Dressmakers

Matchmakers

Marriage brokerage is an old, honored profession, particularly in the East, where it has had its greatest impact and where it still survives today. In ancient China, the *marriage broker* or *go-between* was indispensable, as we learn from *The Book of Odes* (Part I, Book 15, Ode 5):

How do we proceed in splitting firewood?
Without an ax it cannot be done.
How do we proceed in taking a wife?
Without a go-between it cannot be done.

While marriage brokers existed everywhere in the ancient world, it was only in the Far East that they operated lucrative and thriving concerns. In the Near East, the task of arranging marriages very often fell to the *priest*, *astrologer*, or *midwife*. Few of these individuals made actual businesses strictly of matchmaking, but rather added it to their other undertakings. Marriage brokers have been important in the East for centuries. A Chinese law written as late as the beginning of the 18th century A.D. set punishment at 80 blows with a bamboo stick for the father who was negligent in employing a marriage broker for his daughter.

While *matchmakers* in the East have served all classes of people, from the destitute to emperors, their Western counterparts generally did not have access to such a broad or massive public. Typically only a very few matchmakers with sufficiently honorable reputations were able to do business with wealthy or aristocratic families. Within those circles, marriages often became so politically and economically complex that matchmakers could offer little real assistance; Roman Catholic Church leaders, family elders, and ministers of state were consulted instead.

For the general population, matchmaking was more often performed by local busybodies, working without a fee for their own pleasure. Among the well-to-do, dowries were customarily offered to the prospective bridegroom by the bride's family. But countless families of peasants and laborers were barely able to feed themselves, and could not offer dowries. Since the professional matchmaker usually derived a fee for service based on the value of the dowry, this was no place to seek business.

The landed or otherwise propertied heiress was the typical target for European matchmakers. Since there were relatively few of these wealthy young women before the awakening of commercial life during the Renaissance, so there were few matchmakers. But by the 16th century the rising middle class from the growing cities was providing new clients for marriage brokers. Wealthy *merchants* and *shopkeepers* were prime targets for their services; as that class continued to expand phenomenally, so did the brokerage commissions of the marriage-arrangers. Matchmaking was quite popular in Europe between the 15th and 18th centuries. Less prosperous families also began to seek the aid of go-betweens. Where families had little to offer in terms of commission payments, they might provide stores of food or livestock, or sometimes just room and board, while the arrangements were being made. Midwives frequently arranged marriages for peasant families; even those families who could pay nothing at all would frequently resort to the aid of a delegated, supposedly disinterested relative, rather than appear to have no official arranger.

The very existence of this profession indicates the place that women had before recent centuries. The most obvious fact is that women enjoyed a status little better than that of livestock. They were property to be dealt and hopefully profited by. They were often given no say in whom they would marry, and were obliged to fulfill their duties as homemakers and wives wherever they were ultimately "placed." The fact that most marriage brokers in the world were women is also a telling fact. Very few professional opportunities were open to women and, of them, matchmaking was one of the more lucrative and respectable. In the East, go-betweens were usually thought of as very wise, sometimes even sacred women. In Europe, they were seen more as town gossips, who told or even performed colorful stories—all the more attractive in a time when few other forms of entertainment were available, especially in rural areas.

When it had become clear that money could be made from the occupation, a few men entered the field, too. By and large, they were suspected of being too blatantly mercenary and insufficiently sensitive to the delicacy of the situations they sought to mediate. Besides that, they could not invade the confidence of enough housewives to keep properly informed about who was available, at what price, what hidden family disagreements might pressure a father's attitude in one direction or another, and so forth. The only men who seriously rivaled women in this profession were the Catholic priests who, by the 16th century, were trying to enrich their parish coffers by arranging marriages for a fee.

The job of the marriage broker was not a casual one, particularly in the East, where competition was keen and the whole business was better organized. In India, there were different groups of brokers for different castes; this was generally true in China, Japan, and Korea as well, though not in such a formal sense. For the most part, Eastern matchmakers worked regular territories or routes, like the modern-day traveling salesperson or route deliverer. Ideally, territories would not overlap, and cut-throat competition would be kept at a minimum, for the sake of the integrity of the profession. In practice, though, this ideal was impossible to hold to.

When two families became involved in serious negotiations, each one would usually employ a separate go-between. This convention helped prevent either the bride's or the groom's family from being dealt with fraudulently or carelessly. Frequently, one broker would be over-enthusiastic or downright misleading when relating the charms, social status, height, or even age of

Matchmakers long arranged for marriages in the East; here, wedding presents arrive at the bride's home. (From The New America and the Far East, *by G. Waldo Browne, 1901)*

one party to the arrangement. This is understandable, since no marriage meant no commission, just as in real estate today, where a house or property has to be sold before a fee is received. The presence of two brokers, each representing the opposite party, minimized such misrepresentations, which could ultimately affect lives in a very profound way. At the same time, this practice also resulted in the overlap of territories being served by brokers, and in time a great many go-betweens came to be working the same area at the same time.

The matchmaker in the East was usually warmly welcomed in the little villages, where she was regarded as a chief source of entertainment, news, and gritty gossip. The matchmaker played up to this role. She was usually dressed in bright, distinctive clothing, similar to the buffoon-like costuming of stage actresses of the time. She easily obtained free meals and lodging at the home of people seeking either her services or just good, friendly company. Once a broker was employed (usually by the father of the bride), she had serious business to attend to. Her first duty was to compare the horoscopes of the two parties being matched. This was extremely important, for unless the stars were favorable, the matchmaker was obliged to terminate any arrangements for a marriage. First and foremost, the go-between in the Eastern world was—and still is—an astrologer.

After the horoscopes were cleared, the marriage brokers representing the two families might then arrange a meeting between elders of the families. At this meeting, information attained by the brokers would be exchanged. This information included the relative social status, health, and educational backgrounds of the boy and girl. If all went well to this point—that is, if the elders all agreed with the brokers that the match might be appropriate—the bargaining for the dowry began. If this, too, could be agreed upon between both brokers and the families they represented, a date might finally be set for the two partners-for-life to meet. This first meeting was usually at the wedding, although the Japanese often had "seeing sessions," in which the two young people could at least look each other over once in advance.

Many matchmakers in the East were so bogged down with clients that they formed agencies, in which they employed other brokers to go about on their behalf. Many of these agencies were quite extensive and well-organized. *Spies* were sometimes employed to dig out information that might not otherwise be readily made available: The groom's father might be suffering from gambling debts and so anxious to obtain a dowry that he might accept less than he pretended he would; or a so-called "virgin" might actually be otherwise; or a so-called "young man with a future" might in fact be known as a notorious loafer.

Spies would melt into the community and befriend key persons, from whom they might obtain such information. Their findings would ultimately surface during negotiations. After the agreements were all completed, one of the matchmakers sometimes performed the actual wedding ceremony, and often became well loved by the couple. In Japan, the go-between would frequently function later as godfather or godmother to the couple's children, so extending the web of contacts and clients that might one day be passed on to another matchmaker in the family.

Since the breakup of a marriage was considered a blemish on their record, go-betweens would often work hard to keep couples together. They often acted as *marriage counselors* to those whose union had been arranged through their efforts. If matchmakers could not smooth out the problems after some counseling sessions and any number of intervention strategies, they might finally agree to arrange and administer the divorce.

Today, in Eastern countries, there are official marriage bureaus whose counselors help arrange marriages. One such establishment in Tokyo was opened in 1934. Yet the independent marriage broker or agency still represents an extremely influential and important profession. *The*

Illustrated Weekly of India for February 2, 1958, noted that: "Horoscope-agreement must precede matchmaking in most Hindu marriages." This service was then and still is today provided by none other than the professional matchmaker.

Even in the current century, this profession has been extremely powerful, as is clear from the incidents surrounding the institution of the "Sardha Bill" in India in the 1930's. It abolished child marriages—proven to be unhealthful, exploitative, and sometimes fatally dangerous for the physical abuses they sometimes entailed. Fearful of losing business, since most marriages arranged were traditionally of this sort, matchmakers banded together and intentionally misrepresented the law to their clients. They had them believe that after the law went into effect (six months after its passage), *all* marriages would be banned. A torrential flood of marriages ensued over the next six months, leading to a sharp rise in the country's birthrate over the next several years—and ultimately widespread famine.

In the West and in most of the industrialized nations of the world, matchmaking was not a very significant profession after the 18th century. The democratization of society and social reforms leading to individual, civil, and women's rights, all tended to make marriage less of a family affair and more of a romantic one between two people. Nowhere was this more evident than in the United States, a nation noted for the independence and liberality of its citizens. Matchmaking barely drew a breath in the New World, and it all but expired in Western Europe during the 19th century, surviving a little longer in Eastern Europe.

In modern times, however, a new type of matchmaker has emerged, especially in the West, where there is a lack of traditional go-betweens. Dating agencies, which feature sophisticated computer matching and extensive file-keeping systems, have developed since World War II. They were inspired partly by the personal advertisements that were and still are so successful a fea-

ture of many newspapers and magazines. These new matchmakers are not concerned with horoscope readings nor with family traditions or approvals. They are concerned with matching people according to personal appeal and interest. Often, the matching is not even designed with marriage as an end-goal, a rewarding relationship established through dating being the expressed aim of the parties. As a result, the new date-match go-between, while helping lonely or unattached people, does not play the same key role in society as the traditional marriage broker.

Some other modern professions are closely associated with that of the matchmaker. The *marriage counselor* tries to help couples solve marital problems, and thereby avert divorces or separations. The *divorce counselor*, often a specialist *attorney*, helps arrange and negotiate the terms of divorces.

For related occupations in this volume, *Helpers and Aides*, see the following:
   Social Workers

For related occupations in other volumes of the series, see the following:
in *Healers* (forthcoming):
   Midwives
in *Leaders and Lawyers*:
   Lawyers
in *Scholars and Priests* (forthcoming):
   Priests
in *Scientists and Technologists* (forthcoming):
   Astrologers
in *Warriors and Adventurers* (forthcoming):
   Spies

Movers

Movers and *porters* are those who have throughout history physically hauled, moved, or carried things by pushing, pulling, or lifting. In ancient times most of this work was done on a non-professional basis, often by slaves or citizens forced by the state to donate part of their work-year to public works projects. The great pyramids of Egypt were built with considerable assistance from slave porters, who performed the almost inhuman task of moving enormous stone blocks into place. The Great Pyramid of Khufu in Gizeh (near Cairo), which was built in about 2680 B.C., covers some 13 acres at its base and climbs some 482 feet toward the sky. It was called one of the Seven Wonders of the World, partly because people wondered in amazement at the work of those porters—sometimes joined in rows by ankle chains—who had to drag, pull, and push those great masses of solid weight into perfect position. Many of the porters were given heavy doses of raw garlic (a natural anesthetic) to ease the pain that their bodies were forced to endure.

In early China, canal and river barges formed the main basis of cargo transport. Official slaves labored to load and unload these barges at dockside much as *longshore workers* do today. The Chinese slaves had an additional task, though, for they actually hauled the loaded barges along the canal banks until they reached their destinations. Rural peasants frequently paid their government taxes by acting as such unpaid transport workers—called "trackers"—between the seasons of sowing and harvesting.

In the Greek and Roman civilizations, slave porters were put to work hauling produce to markets and heavy building materials to the sites of public projects. The Romans sent porters along on military campaigns to haul supplies and provisions, and even to cart troop commanders.

Many porters also worked carrying other human beings. The most popular method of doing this was to use a litter or a sedan-chair. The litter was a couch with curtains, and the sedan-chair was a throne-like seat. Both were attached to two parallel poles. These were

These workers loading boats for Queen Hatshepsut's expedition to the land of Punt were among the many laborers who made Egypt's greatness possible. (Authors' archives, second century B.C.)

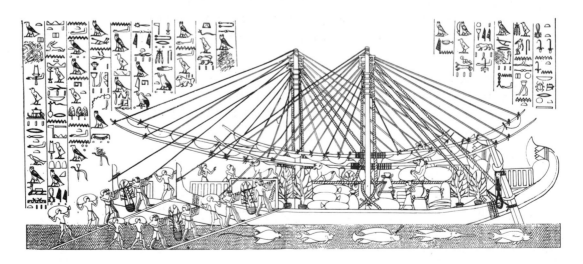

In mountainous parts of the world, as here in China, porters often bore human cargo in makeshift chairs on their backs. (From Museum of the American China Trade)

carried by as few as two people, particularly in Europe, or as many as eight, notably in China. *Litter-bearers* worked all over the globe, in the Old World and the New. They were very widely used in China, where even the carpentry specifications for a building sometimes indicated the angle of a slope by whether litter-bearers could hold their arms straight or would need to bend them to negotiate the stairs. Litter-bearers were equally important in the Roman Empire. There the major cities were so crowded that in some of them, including Rome itself, wheeled vehicles were barred in the daytime. As a result the idle rich turned to litter-bearers, often their own slaves or *servants*, to carry them around town.

In many lands the porter's life was made a little easier by the use of wheeled vehicles. Among the many variations were a two-wheeled cart pulled by a porter holding onto parallel bars, a vehicle variously called a *roulette* or a *jinrickshaw* (*rickshaw*, for short); a similar cart with the addition of a sail (a Chinese specialty); and a two-wheeled cart affixed to a bicycle, a modern variation.

Traditional porters continue to operate in some Eastern cities, and did so in Europe at least through the 18th century.

Some porters simply carried other human beings, sometimes "piggyback," at other times in chairlike backpacks. In some parts of the world, notably South America, porters using backpacks to carry people or goods strapped the load on with a leather band around their foreheads. The device cut so deeply into the flesh that, even when they were not working, these porters were instantly identifiable as to occupation. Often a particular family, tribe, or caste was assigned the portering duties within society. People in this occupation received little status anywhere in the world.

The earliest professional carriers of goods were the *postal carriers* employed by monarchs, governments, and private companies. From China to England these people set out on the official business of carrying important messages from one point to another. Along the way, they sometimes agreed to transport light goods headed for the same destination, thus increasing their incomes. At the same time, they ran the risk of losing their postal positions by taking these extra assignments, since all such contracts were supposed to be made only through the *dispatchers*, who would take the greater portion of the profit from the arrangement.

In Europe, the Middle Ages were marked by stagnating commerce, due partly to the poor condition of roadways, but mostly to the lack of interaction and exchange between neighboring towns, to say nothing of neighboring and distant kingdoms. An erratic, confusing, and expensive system of tolls, duties, and taxes applied as a carrier moved through many tiny, independent political units in traveling even the shortest of distances. Traveling was also dangerous. Without bank notes or letters of credit, people had to carry gold, silver, and other precious mediums of exchange with them. And there were always *highwaymen* prowling the roads eager to relieve people of their precious goods. Along with the general lack of law and order outside of the main cities and manors, there was little push for regular or large-scale trade—or for the establishment of moving, hauling, and carrying professions.

With the revival of trade in the Renaissance, all this began to change. The expansion of commerce during this period and the increasing sophistication of banking—with letters of credit, bills of exchange, and the like—made it less important for merchants to personally do their own hauling. They were able, then, to enlist the labors of *carters* and *haulers*, who transported merchandise for a fee.

A standard contract known as the *letter of carriage* came into existence to seal arrangements between merchants and professional haulers. One such letter

The leather strap on this bearer's forehead made a permanent impression after a lifetime of carrying heavy loads. (From Voyage pittoresque et archéologique dans la partie la plus intéressante du Mexique, *by C. Nebel)*

hints at how dangerous and expensive the business of moving merchandise was:

Odon Baghasque, carrier, promises to Aubert Bagnaret to transport at his own cost, including tolls, with risks of robbery falling to Aubert, six bales from Marseilles to Troyes, from the day of this act to Christmas, in exchange for a horse given by Aubert.

Most of these early carriers and movers did not actually make full-time businesses out of their hauls. They were often adventurous *farmers* looking for some extra earnings during the off-season. Many carriers were found among the highway *robbers* themselves—people who knew the roads and the pitfalls of travel well enough to realize a regular profit from making such runs. They could usually be found slinking in and out of inns and taverns along the roadways. They earned either a wage or, more likely, an agreed-upon gift—food, a wagon, or a horse—for honest work, while at the same time always on the lookout for easy marks for their familiar skills of thievery. Some of the more fortunate carriers had a mule or sometimes even a horse to get them where they were going, but most of them had only their legs.

By the end of the 16th century wagon loads of cargo began moving along improved roadways throughout Western Europe. This was the beginning of regular moving and hauling organizations. Most of these were operated by *innkeepers* and *roadhouse proprietors*, who dispatched teams of *wagoners* and carters to carry goods from town to town. By then, more and more horses were appearing in Europe—larger, stronger, and faster ones. The slower mule teams were soon replaced, as the business became swifter and more reliable. Innkeepers were the most logical proprietors of these moving and hauling operations. They had stalls for housing the horses or mules, yards for storing the wagons and carts, and facilities for feeding and lodging the thieves and toughs who frequented such places and might be talked into becoming drivers or porters.

As inland moving became an established business, and overseas transportation opened up a new flow of goods entering and leaving dockyards, porters came to be recognized as a distinct class of laborers. Needed by both government and business for the loading and unloading of goods, and for the delivery of merchandise to residences and business establishments within the cities, they first came to prominence in the great European ports. It did not take long for porters to gather into associations that closely resembled contemporary labor unions.

The City Porters Association of London was founded in 1579. By the beginning of the 17th century a complex organization of porters existed in that city. The *Aliens' Porters* typically unloaded, weighed, and dispersed goods that arrived at London docks of entry from foreign countries. The *Tacklehouse Porters* (those who worked in buildings equipped with tackle, such as ropes and pulleys, to help in unloading ships) and *Ticket Porters* (those licensed by the city) worked wharves and sometimes even acted as *warehouse keepers* for companies maintaining waterside establishments.

Of course, some companies chose to employ their own salaried porters rather than free roamers, who could not always be trusted with expensive merchandise. Nonetheless, most merchants found it most convenient to use the city-licensed porters, who would work both the wharves and the in-city locations of loading and unloading. Such porters displayed tickets to prove that they were licensed city laborers, thus reducing the risk of handing over one's cargo to an imposter, who might haul it away and never be seen again.

If a porter stole or damaged a merchant's goods, he was held personally liable for the losses so incurred. Since porters typically were drawn from the poorest class in society, however, a merchant would be fortunate indeed to ever recover more than a fraction of his loss. To discourage merchants from using foreign or unlicensed porters, porters' fellowships were organized to pool

In England, ticket porters were licensed and required to wear their badge of certification around their necks. (Authors' archives, 1747)

liability. The fellowship system, by pooling the individual liabilities of its contributing members, offered a sort of mutual insurance to the merchant to cover the lost, stolen, or damaged goods.

The 17th and 18th centuries marked the heyday of porters in the pre-industrial nations of the world. Some of the portering work was carried on in a very casual manner. If a ship came in, a group of *farmers*, *shopkeepers* and derelicts might assemble to earn a day's wage—these were the so-called *day laborers*. They then returned to their regular vocations or roles.

In China, porters were still used not only to load and unload barges, but also to transport passengers in rickshaws or other forms of carriages or seats. *Coolies* were seen everywhere in the streets of China's cities, lifting carriages on bamboo poles. Inside the carriages were officials and travelers. The one-wheeled rickshaw allowed a single porter to handle a passenger—or even two—increasing the profit in such trade. Chinese porters of heavy materials or goods balanced them on wooden planks that sat upon their shoulders.

In Asia, South America, and Africa, it was common for porters to frequent dangerous mountain passes. There they would unload pack animals and escort them along the mountain ways that they made it their business to know thoroughly—all the time carrying the cargo that the animals could not bear on such treacherous paths. Finally, they would reload the beasts of burden on the other side of the mountain. One 17th-century adventurer traveling through Kashmir, north of India, reportedly employed no fewer than 15,000 porters to help him along the way. Although some were slaves, many others, it was noted, were "attracted by the alluring pay of ten crowns per hundred pounds in weight." In Brazil, prisoners were used as porters to haul water and as replacements for mules in pulling carts.

In the commercial centers of the world, however, porters were no longer slaves and seldom prisoners. By the 17th century they were workers typically employed in a regular, sometimes organized, laboring vocation. So thriving was the business of hauling, carrying, and

Sedan chairs and rickshaws were still in widespread use in Hong Kong in the early 20th century. (From The New America and the Far East, *by G. Waldo Browne, 1901)*

delivering, that an increasing number of laborers took on the general title of porter. It had become a full-time and sometimes even lucrative profession, even if it never attained great social esteem. In some cities, individual porters might gain such success in their work that they could leave it altogether and take on the more enviable position of independent *porterage contractors*, who hired other porters to do the physical work that they had only to arrange. At the height of portering as a regular profession, the hardy laboring porters came to earn respectable livings among wage-earners. One account of the lot of the licensed London porter illustrates how far along the vocation had progressed by 1747:

> The Use of these [city porters] every Gentleman Merchant, and Trader knows; but they differ greatly, according to the Nature of the Business they follow; some being for downright Labour and heavy Work in various Shapes, others middling, and some very little or none, as those belonging to the Inns of Court, Companies and Noblemen; but most of them get good livelihoods, and some live very handsomely.

Despite the improved lot of porters, they were generally despised in the commercial world, owing mostly to their crude manners and frequent involvement in gaming, thievery, and other licentious behaviors. One observer, after his arrival in London in 1765, listed porters along with sailors and "day labourers" as "the mob" that made the city a most disagreeable and uncomfortable place to visit or live in for a regular gentleman. They were, he insisted, "as insolent a rabble as can be met with in countries without law or police." Wherever porters congregated—usually along docksides and at dubious inns—decent folk were careful to stay away. Even those who enlisted porters' services—often reluctantly—complained endlessly about missing merchandise and mindless acts of carelessness. Licensed porters were, however, engaged by the early insurance company-sponsored firefighting companies to remove valuable goods from burning buildings. Their label or ticket was prominently displayed to prevent their arrest for looting.

In London, where porters were better organized and protected than anywhere else in the world, these workers faced long and bitter legal battles against them during the second half of the 18th century. The *wharfingers*, who operated or leased tacklehouses and import businesses on river fronts and at ports of entry, led the attack. Thomas Bolt, occupying premises at Fresh Wharf, Dice and Smart's Quays, refused to allow authorized Ticket Porters to handle a shipment of hemp in 1791. A long court struggle ensued. At one point, when Bolt was ordered by the Court of Aldermen to use the licensed porters, he effectively blocked the entire dock with his barges, to the dismay of the *oystermen*, who could not put to shore with their catch. Threats of violence from both sides made the situation a potentially explosive one. Still, it was only the beginning.

The wharfingers were soon joined by shopkeepers and merchants in town, and by innkeepers, in their attempt to break the hold that the city's porters had gotten on local businesses. Shopkeepers, like the wharfingers, insisted that they were better off employing their own laborers to handle whatever porterage was necessary. As professional carting establishments multiplied, *drivers* and their helpers were doing the loading and unloading of their own shipments. Often, professional porters were not really needed. The innkeepers who operated such cargo transport enterprises complained bitterly about having to pay high rates to Ticket Porters, while their own drivers sat idly by—and while their rented rooms were filled with eager day laborers, who would do carrying and loading at a fraction of the cost.

It was not easy to do away with the porters—particularly where they were organized. Regardless of how crude, careless, dishonest, and expensive they may sometimes have been, they still performed tasks that few other people wished to endure.

A Parisian porter in 1782 bewailed how his occupation demanded that he routinely lift and haul "loads that would kill a horse." By the beginning of the 19th century, it was the horse that was relieving porters of their most trying chores. Wagons pulled by horses had largely replaced porters in Europe by the 1820's for most hauling. Drivers of these wagons had begun to take on the short-haul loading and unloading portering duties, as the occupation's protective associations began to wane.

The "human beast of burden" had not yet disappeared though. With the Industrial Revolution well in gear, horses and wagons proved to be more cost-efficient and capable of carrying heavier loads than men were. But industrialization also created great demand for coal and other underground minerals and ores needed by the new factories. The mines had become essential to the functioning of the industrialized world, particularly England, whose factories were leading the way. But horses and wagons could not haul heavy carts of coal from the depths of the pits up shafts too small for a man to stand upright in. Boys, women, and girls were pressed to do the job, acting as *pushers* or *hurriers*, as they were known in the British mines.

The Children's Employment Commission published investigative findings in 1842 that illustrated the nature of the hurriers' task: "A girdle is put around the naked waist, to which a chain from the carriage is hooked and passed between the legs, and the boys crawl on their hands and knees, drawing the carriage after them." The same commission also reported on the wretched labor of young girl pushers in the West Riding:

Chained, belted, harnessed like dogs in a go-cart, back saturated with wet, and more than half naked—crawling upon their hands and feet, and dragging their heavy loads behind them—they present an appearance indescribably disgusting and unnatural.

The days of the pushers and hurriers finally ended not through legislation or corporate pangs of conscience, but only when mechanized and motorized engines finally replaced them. By 1842 carts had been placed on rails, so that drivers could pull them. These drivers were usually teenaged boys harnessed together in teams of two, typically working from 2 A.M. until 8 or 10 P.M., six days a week. A few years later, though, motorized carts were on the scene and the drivers quietly disappeared.

With the invention of motorized vehicles, conveyor belts, lifting devices, and the like, there was no longer much need for porters, carriers, and haulers. Perhaps the last of the great haulers were the *icemen* of the late 19th and early 20th centuries, who ran up and down flights of stairs in city buildings to deliver heavy chunks of ice to customers employing the latest fad—the icebox. Even after the development of motorized trucks, icemen still had to cart their heavy cargo from truck to icebox, which was usually no small chore.

In today's modern world of engines, trucks, and machines, only a few carriers are needed and they are usually aided to some extent by devices such as two-wheeled hand trucks, roller conveyors, or even motorized fork lifts. Some porters—though far fewer than years ago—work in transportation terminals and hotels, helping travelers with their luggage, with tips supplementing their modest salaries.

Longshore workers load and unload freighters much as the London Tacklehouse and Aliens' Porters did in the 17th and 18th centuries. They have, however, been hard hit by the modern use of containers to hold goods on ships; these massive boxcars are unloaded by crane in far less time, and—more to the point—require far fewer laborers. The number of longshore workers has, as a result, dropped sharply in recent years. Those who remain, however, earn better money, as well as pensions and medical benefits, and are protected by unions that

In the great warehouses of London, winches and pulleys were used as aids for hauling heavy cargo up several stories. (By Gustave Doré, from London: A Pilgrimage, *1872)*

are even stronger than the London porters' fellowships once were. *Truck drivers* usually help load and unload their trailers, but most of their work is in driving the rigs.

Perhaps the heaviest carrying work today is done by furniture, appliance, and household *movers*. Usually working in teams of either two or three, they have to load heavy pieces of cargo into vans, drive them to the destined site, unload them, and carry each piece or package into its proper place. This can often be backbreaking work, when pianos, couches, refrigerators, and other heavy one-piece items have to be physically carried up winding stairs and deposited perfectly in place.

Although movers operated vans even when horse-drawn wagons were the only such vehicles available, it has only been since World War II that their services have been in great demand. Rising populations and consumer-item manufacturing have been important factors in this rise. Even more important, however, has been the sharp increase in the number of people moving from one geographical location to another in industrialized nations. Large corporations often transfer employees to new locations and frequently pay the movers' fees. Many

Licensed carters made a killing on May Day, the traditional moving day in early New York City. (By Alfred Fredericks, from Harper's Weekly, *April 30, 1859)*

large moving corporations now provide special services, such as packing and unpacking entire warehouses and households for their customers. Independent movers often deal exclusively in short-haul and local moves.

Of course, in the less-developed countries of the world, porters, carriers, and haulers are still used much as they were the world over before the Industrial Revolution. Icemen are very prosperous in India today, as are barge loaders and unloaders throughout Southeast Asia. Human carriers are still used to transport goods over rugged terrain in Africa, and through mountain passes in South America and Tibet.

For related occupations in this volume, *Helpers and Aides*, see the following:
    Drivers
    Firefighters

For related occupations in other volumes of the series, see the following:
in *Builders*:
    Construction Laborers
in *Communicators*:
    Messengers and Couriers
in *Financiers and Traders*:
    Bankers and Financiers
    Insurers
    Merchants and Shopkeepers
in *Harvesters*:
    Farmers
    Fishers
in *Manufacturers and Miners* (forthcoming):
    Miners and Quarriers
in *Restaurateurs and Innkeepers* (forthcoming):
    Innkeepers
in *Warriors and Adventurers* (forthcoming):
    Robbers and Other Criminals
    Sailors

Private Guards and Detectives

Before modern times, *bodyguards*, private *watchmen* and private *criminal investigators* were usually military personnel. Sometimes *political leaders* and *legislators*—such as Roman *senators* or English circuit *judges*—acted like *detectives* in trying to obtain evidence in relation to particular criminal cases. Kings and queens had private bodyguards, as did some other wealthy or important individuals, but they were typically *soldiers* or *knights*.

In the 19th century, the growth of industrial cities placed greater demands on the law enforcement profession. England was one of the earliest countries to employ public police forces. Later in the century, they began to use *plainclothes officers* as detectives to try to obtain information that had bearing on criminal cases. In time, these officers came to constitute a separate detective force. *Private investigators* did much the same type of work, but were directly responsible to the individuals who employed them privately to pursue such matters. The fictional character Sherlock Holmes is probably the best-known prototype of the private investigator. Detectives and investigators became necessary as criminal legislation grew increasingly complex and as evidence in court proceedings had to be more thoroughly analyzed and qualified. Before the 19th century, circumstantial evidence—that is, coincidence rather than direct observation of fact—or even wild accusations lodged by persons of influence were often enough to convict the suspect. Today, great care must be taken to qualify such evidence and accusations in order for them to be even admissible in many courts of law. *Public in-*

Monarchs, nobles, and wealthy notables often employed private guards, like this Tiger Guard from China, to ensure their safety. (From The New America and the Far East, *by G. Waldo Browne, 1901)*

Private detectives often employed disguises in their work; this one removes a toupee to reveal his identity. (Advertising woodcut for The Ticket-of-Leave Man, *London and New York, 1863)*

vestigators are commissioned to make such investigations as are deemed necessary to a given case, but persons who can afford to, sometimes wish to hire private investigators as well.

Private guards to protect individuals as well as private property became regular professionals as the industrial age created greater opportunities and stimuli for criminal acts against both. From the mid-19th century on, private guard companies like Pinkerton's in the United States were used to break union strikes and protect non-strikers. Private bodyguards have been employed by people of wealth, position, and fame for at least the last hundred years to protect them against crime and personal dangers, particularly in public places. Guards and night watchmen are often hired to protect businesses and estates from burglary and trespassing. Armed agents drive armored cars that make pickups and deliveries of large amounts of cash and valuables from banks, jewelry stores, and large cash businesses. Organized crime leaders retain members of their own organizations as personal bodyguards; they also commission independent or affiliated *hit men* to assassinate their foes.

Generally speaking, the more valuable the property or person being protected by independent guards, the higher their commissions, but also the greater the danger involved. Guards working for agencies, however—as most armored car guards do—typically earn only a modest wage for the considerable peril they face. In such cases, it is only the agency itself that profits greatly from the dangers its employees face every day. Because of the precarious nature of the work and the need to be expert with firearms, former police officers or military personnel are the preferred job candidates.

For related occupations in this volume, *Helpers and Aides*, see the following:
    Drivers

For related occupations in other volumes of the series, see the following:
in *Leaders and Lawyers*:
    Lawyers
    Judges
    Police Officers
    Political Leaders
in *Manufacturers and Miners* (forthcoming):
    Factory Workers
in *Warriors and Adventurers* (forthcoming):
    Robbers and Other Criminals
    Soldiers

Sanitation Workers

The concept of sanitation is a relatively new one, historically speaking. In ancient times, people did not see the connection between the rapid spreading of epidemic diseases and such everyday realities as rats, mosquitoes, and filth in the streets and at home. Instead, disease was considered a sign of displeasure sent down from the heavens—an instance of divine wrath, judgment, or sometimes just plain harassment on the part of the patron deity of an enemy tribe or kingdom. The Greeks are the first people known to have been concerned with cleanliness at all, but they focused mostly on personal hygiene.

Of course, ancient cities did not have throw-away cans, bottles, or boxes to contend with. As is still true today in very poor countries, what was discarded by the wealthy was almost always salvaged and put to use by others.

And even the relatively few cities existing at the time were only large towns by modern standards. In short, ancient cities were hardly the receptacles of garbage and litter that modern ones are. Rome was, however, large enough and sufficiently troubled by sanitation to undertake the construction of remarkably sophisticated and effective sewer systems. The Roman Commissioner of Sewers might even be regarded as the first professional *sanitation engineer*.

In the latter part of the Middle Ages, more serious sanitation problems developed. Plagues and epidemics had been a way of life for centuries, culminating in the massive outbreak of bubonic plague, called the Black Death, in the mid-14th century, which killed possibly one-quarter or more of Europe's population.

As Renaissance towns began to crop up with the new activity in trade, city households and shops became more and more numerous. Periodic famines drove countless numbers of desperate peasants into the cities in search of some kind of work or shelter, or just some daily bread. Cities were soon vastly overcrowded. Being poorly planned, they had narrow, crooked streets, no sewer systems, no running water, and few sources of truly pure drinking water.

Soon the cramped streets were strewn with the garbage of households and shops, there being no refuse collectors or specially designated dumping grounds. *Butchers* even tossed animal flesh into the streets and the rivers, attracting rats and insects that carried deadly diseases. All kinds of animal droppings fouled the streets, too, for most urban dwellers still lived as they had in the country, leaving domestic pigs, hens, dogs, and cats to roam freely. And there was even human waste in the streets, for citizens routinely emptied their chamber pots from second-story windows into the sea of filth and stench in the sorry street below.

It was not until the scientific discoveries of bacteria, other microorganisms, and parasite cycles that authorities began to associate this unattended refuse and waste with diseases and plagues. It eventually became apparent that the fortunate home owner or shopkeeper who occupied premises on the waterfront was not as fortunate as he had always thought, in having the same ready supply of water available for both drinking and sewage disposal.

The technology to make cities more sanitary was slow in developing, however. London had drainage systems as early as the 13th century A.D., though dumping waste into them was supposedly illegal before 1815. Paris had sewers in the 15th century, but even at the end of the 19th century only some 5 percent of the city's private dwellings were hooked into the system.

Although it took cities a long time to apply sanitary engineering systems, other more immediate measures were taken to help alleviate the problem of disease-breeding refuse. By the 17th century most major European cities had ordinances stipulating how frequently waste could be thrown into the streets, and during which hours—the aim being to save pedestrians from being directly splashed.

London was one of the first cities to actually employ *sanitation workers* to clean up some of the mess that had for so many centuries been taken for granted. In the 17th century *night-soil men* went about the city's streets with buckets and carts during the night-hours, cleaning up whatever accumulations they happened upon. Similar efforts were made in Paris, and later in New York and Boston. Refuse collection—disposing of the garbage and litter from personal households—was not a major occupation at that time, though, nor did it become so until the appearance of 20th-century consumer societies. Individuals, by and large, found their own means of garbage disposal—what little need was felt for such activity.

In general, sanitation in the major cities was improved not so much by the dutiful efforts of the night-soil men as by improvements in urban living conditions. They may be noted from an account given in 1819 by one Dr. Marshall,

London dustmen wore distinctive garb, notably the fan-tail hat that protected their neck and shoulders from the elements. (By W. H. Pyne, from Costume of Great Britain, *1808)*

who described to a parliamentary committee how much better off London was in terms of disease control than it had been just a short time earlier:

> . . . if any causes could have contributed to the immunity we enjoy from the plague and bad fevers, they are to be found in the greater cleanliness and less crowded state of the inhabitants, with the widening of the streets, and the better and more general construction of common sewers and drains, to which may be added the profusion of water now distributed through the metropolis.

The Industrial Revolution made cities even more crowded, and sanitation became a greater matter of concern than ever before. The English were the first to create a filthy factory world, but they also took unprecedented initiatives to tend to sanitation. *Nightmen* cleaned the streets, aided by *scavengers*, who were often young boys without homes or shelter, seeking a few pennies of pay for their labors. The Paving and Improvement Acts, which had begun in 1762, led to the appointment of Paving Commissioners, who were responsible for providing street scavenging, constructing and improving sewers, and the periodic flushing of mid-street "kennels," into which *street sweepers* pushed sludge and debris. The British sanitation system was exemplary, and as one observer noted in 1787, "is the admiration of all Europe and far exceeds anything of the kind in the modern world." Not only were the streets "better and more regularly cleansed" as yet another observer remarked, but efforts were even made toward "washing the filth out of the kennels and common shoars . . . ."

Chimney-sweeping became an active and infamous profession in England early in the 18th century. By 1817 there were some 400 master *chimney-sweeps* and about 1,000 apprentices in England. While the masters lined up jobs and arranged contracts for cleaning chimneys, the actual labor was performed almost exclusively by small boys—usually orphans or children whose poverty-stricken parents had sold their persons or services. Some children may even have been kidnapped by the master chimney-sweeps, who sometimes also employed their own offspring—girls as well as boys.

Few jobs could have been as unimaginably horrible as that of the impish chimney-sweeps. When they were not using their bodies to scale sooty chimneys, they were put to the task of "crying" for work at the doors of the well-to-do, or else passing out handbills in the street advertising: "Small boys for small flues." Masters had to force them up their first chimneys by sticking their feet with pins or by lighting a fire beneath them as they began their reluctant climbs. "If the Chimneys happen to be too small," it was reported in 1788, "they call the Boys down, strip them, and beat them, and force them up again, by which means they become crippled." A master sweep remarked in the same year that, according to his

calculations, a chimney 12-inch square was sufficient for a boy of seven to easily climb. But there was not always enough space to crawl through, and many a lad suffocated to death in the line of duty, while still others were fatally burned.

In 1817, a gentleman offered this description of the failed attempt to have his chimney swept:

> There was a hole made in the side for the boy to go up, and the boy was repeatedly driven in at the hole, but the mortar and soot fell in such great lumps upon his head, and with such force, that if he had not had a cap upon his head it would have been broken. Upon seeing the boy writhing in order to get into the chimney, and being satisfied he could not conveniently get up, although the man who was his master being without feeling seemed to say it was mere idleness in the boy, and that he would force the boy up, I would not suffer it, and the chimney was not swept.

Remarking on claims that the boys had their growth stunted for this sordid occupation, a surgeon of the time had this to say:

The knees and ankle-joints mostly become deformed, in the first instance, from the position they are obliged to put them in, in order to support themselves, not only while climbing up the chimney, but more particularly so in that of coming down, when they rest solely on the lower extremities, the arms being used for scraping and sweeping down the soot in the meantime: this in addition to that of carrying heavy loads confirms the complaint.

Most sanitation occupations of the 19th century were related to street cleaning. The scavengers, nightmen, and street sweepers were generally recruited from the lower classes of society. Often these jobs—performed during late night or early morning hours—were taken on as only part-time ventures to supplement more regular employment. For the most part, only those in dire need would resort to such sordid labor. Some street cleaners were social outcasts, drunkards, or others who could not otherwise find suitable employment. *Supervisors* often complained that they slept on the job, or were otherwise remiss in carrying out their duties.

Paid officials were appointed in London to oversee the work of nightmen, and to mete out fines and punishments if they were caught shortcutting their tasks by doing such things as dumping their carts on back streets instead of hauling them to specified dumping grounds. For the most part, though, street cleaners got their jobs done and, in the process, helped make modern cities sanitary and healthful. Many were hard-working, honest people who were forced by any of a variety of situations into accepting this unheralded occupation.

With the mass production of tons of cheap, consumable items and with the introduction of disposable containers and convenience products, a virtually new "consumer society" has been created in the 20th century, especially since World War II in the industrialized nations. These consumers have created a virtual world of litter. Households, restaurants, hospitals, institutional cafeterias—all throw away tons of "garbage" every day, in the form of paper, cardboard, plastic, and the like. *Refuse collectors* have become increasingly necessary for the ordinary sanitation and functioning of modern society. In 1981 it was reported that "Britons are throwing out more and more for the *dustman*—the equivalent of 322 Kg of rubbish per person, an increase of 10 Kg between 1979 and 1980. . . . In London, most waste was collected in Westminster: 154,000 tonnes, enough to fill the Houses of Parliament."

Garbage collectors are typically public employees in large cities, but are usually employed by private companies in the less-populated suburbs or rural areas. In either case, their services have become so indispensable that their standard of living has risen considerably, through massive unionization and other forms of organization. Garbage strikes have proven very effective in helping them attain greater prosperity and better working conditions. But being more vital to society, they have also increasingly been held up to scrutiny and abuse. A British journalist noted in September 1980, that dustmen in Peterborough, Cambridgeshire, were demanding security for themselves against "householders who are angry about the erratic emptying

Convicts like this chain gang of Blacks were sometimes employed to do street-cleaning duties. (From Frank Leslie's Illustrated Weekly, late 1870's)

Garbage collectors often dumped their haul onto barges, where ragpickers searched for possible items of value. (By Stanley Fox, from Harper's Weekly, September 29, 1866)

of bins." The report continues: "Recently, a resident armed with a cosh pursued a burly dustman down a street. Another refuse collector was taken to hospital for seven stitches in a face wound after he was attacked with a knife." A spokesman of Britain's National Union of Public Employees noted that some of the workers were being pushed around in public places and even confronted at their homes.

The duties of *street cleaners*, *sewer cleaners*, and garbage collectors have been made considerably easier since the invention of the motor vehicle. Much less "hands-on" work is now involved in these tasks. While pickup trucks at first were used to simply haul refuse, special garbage disposal trucks now crush and compact deposited rubbish so that even fewer trips have to be made to the city or town dump. Street-cleaning and snow-plowing are now done with large trucks specifically designed or adapted for those purposes, so street sanitation workers are relieved of broom and shovel—as well as aching backs and calluses. The mechanization of street sanitation and refuse removal has allowed cities to maintain relatively low payrolls, even in the face of a world with ever-growing amounts of waste, and larger, more populous communities to be cleaned.

The 20th century has seen the rise of other sanitation occupations which, while not nearly as significant as that of the garbage collectors, have also played a role in the sanitation and cleaning of places where people live and work. *Window washers* began to specialize in their unique service after World War I, when many new buildings were being built so high that no one else dared to hang out the windows to clean them. Contemporary cities feature many skyscrapers that are almost all glass, but without actual windows that open and close. These are cleaned by teams of window washers, who employ safety belts and movable platforms in their hazardous occupation.

The interiors of public and private buildings—business offices, libraries, institutions, banks, schools, and even private homes—are cleaned by *janitors* or *custodians*. Though many work after regular business hours, some work during the normal daytime hours of operation. In the 18th and 19th centuries, office-cleaning was typically

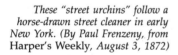

These "street urchins" follow a horse-drawn street cleaner in early New York. (By Paul Frenzeny, from Harper's Weekly, *August 3, 1872)*

done by the workers themselves, such as *clerks*, *secretaries*, *teachers*, and *nurses*. The increase in building sizes and professional specialization in the 20th century led to the allocation of cleaning chores to a special group of laborers.

In some cases, rising crime in the cities also led many businesses to employ *guards* or *watchmen* to keep an eye on the security of the building. Often, these people became *caretakers* as well, making building repairs when necessary and sometimes carrying out cleaning chores. Modern custodians act as cleaners, repairers, and even security guards. The *maintenance person* also performs duties similar to those of the custodian, but is typically more involved in repairs, carpentry, painting, and the like than in regular cleaning. Building *superintendents* often do some or all these things, particularly in apartment complexes where immediate attention must frequently be given to plumbing, electrical, or boiler troubles.

The janitor is the person most closely associated with sanitation in buildings. This occupation includes the regular cleaning of dust and dirt, the disposal of garbage, and sometimes the keeping up of immediately surrounding courts and yards, although this latter responsibility more formally falls to the *groundskeeper*. The janitor's work may also involve more specialized duties, such as the disinfecting of special wards in hospitals or laboratories, floor-waxing, carpet-cleaning, and window-washing. In hotels and motels, *chambermaids*, janitors, and *housekeepers* all share in the cleaning of private rooms and common halls, rooms, and lobbies. They change linens, make up beds, vacuum clean carpets, and disinfect toilet areas. Janitoring comprises the one sanitation occupation that is commonly open to women. In most other categories, and especially in refuse collection and street-sweeping, women are rarely employed. Women janitors—sometimes called *matrons*—are very common, though, and in many places far outnumber men.

The pay for janitors varies widely, but is generally not considerable. The job carries with it the same social stigma that most sanitation jobs have always had, and only people who cannot get other sorts of work generally enter this field. For that reason, it has long been a popular source of income for women and handicapped individuals, as well as ethnic and racial minorities. Many people work at janitoring positions as part-time employees, and many are hard-working and honest. In times of economic decline, many well-educated, highly skilled people also resort to such work. Janitors are employed by private cleaning companies that send them out on different jobs as contracts are made, as well as by institutions that retain them as regular in-house employees. Some people have, however, established small, independent cleaning businesses, operating primarily in the suburbs.

The highest level of sanitation work involves the professional attention of *engineers* who direct the building of sewers, dams, and reservoirs. The executive *building-maintenance supervisors* are in charge of the proper cleaning of a particular place, but also of the proper functioning of its often complex plumbing, electrical, and mechanical systems and devices.

Sanitation poses a special problem when related to the disposal of industrial waste and air and water pollution. Specially trained engineers, as well as "mop-up" teams, are employed to deal with these complex problems. Oil spills, radiation leaks, and chemical contamination offer hazardous situations that can be dealt with effectively only by highly trained and knowledgeable sanitation crews.

For related occupations in this volume, *Helpers and Aides*, see the following:

Exterminators and Pest Controllers
Servants and Other Domestic Laborers

For related occupations in other volumes of the series, see
the following:

in *Builders*:
  Carpenters
  Plumbers
in *Manufacturers and Miners* (forthcoming):
  Mechanics and Repairers
  Power and Fuel Merchants
in *Restaurateurs and Innkeepers* (forthcoming):
  Innkeepers
in *Scientists and Technologists* (forthcoming):
  Engineers

Servants and Other Domestic Laborers

In ancient times, virtually all *servants* were slaves owned outright by their masters. Many were born to slave parents in the households where they would spend the rest of their lives as servants, if they were not traded to another owner. Many others were captured in war and brought back enslaved. In some lands free citizens could be reduced to slave status if they were unable to pay their debts or taxes; sometimes children were sold into slavery by destitute parents. In early China, relatives of convicted criminals were often made slaves; they became the property of the government, though some were later sold to private owners. These servants supplied the domestic labor to run upper-class households, performing work that, in lower-class households, was generally performed by *housewives*.

Many slave-servants in these early times were well cared for. They lived and worshipped with their owners and so enjoyed far more protection and more comfortable surroundings than the peasants of the time. In Egypt, servants generally lived in small huts close to their workplaces, near the stables or kitchen area, for example. Highly regarded senior servants sometimes had their own small houses within the family compound. In China, many government-owned servants became so rich that it caused a public scandal. These servants were entitled to draw from public supplies of produce and goods for their own upkeep. It turned out that many so-called servants had actually done no work at all. And many had gathered fortunes a hundred times the amount a peasant could earn.

But even slaves who lived comfortable lives were not free. Though household servants were generally not required to do heavy labor—at least not compared to the work of slaves who built Egypt's pyramids or China's Great Wall—their work was still monotonous and not of their own choosing. There were reduced to the status of mere chattel (property).

In early Egypt, servants of the pharaoh or even those of powerful nobles were sometimes buried alive with their masters when the masters died. Supposedly, they did so willingly and even gladly, since they considered their masters to be gods who would speak well of them in the next world. This practice was evident as late as the 14th

This white-kilted Egyptian scribe seems to be conducting a roll call of these Black slaves with their families. (From History of Egypt, *by Clara Erskine Clement, 1903)*

century A.D. among some Native South and Central Americans. In some cultures, representations of a great man's followers—not actual people—were buried; in China, for example, whole armies of statues have been uncovered from royal tombs.

In ancient Mesopotamia, servants acted as *tasters*, sampling food and wine before it was offered to their masters or as sacrifices to the gods. This was to ensure that if it was bad or poisoned, the servant would be the one to get sick or die, thus protecting the master.

In Greco-Roman times, servants continued to be mostly slaves. Even a Greek family of modest means might have three servants, while the rich would have a good many more. While the practice was pervasive, many Greeks felt uneasy about slaves. Even Plato, who assumed that slavery was natural, commented in his *Republic*: "A slave is an embarrassing possession, the distinction between man and slave being a difficult one and slaves should be well-treated and not abused or insulted."

Surely many slaves were abused, human nature being what it is, but in these times a different attitude toward slavery seemed to be developing. Slaves began to accumulate status and rights, some formal, others informal. By law, someone who killed a slave was charged with manslaughter, while those harassing slaves could be fined. Within the family, new slaves were greeted by celebrations with confetti, and household slave-servants joined in with the family both in religious observances and in cultural events like the theater. One Greek observer described the situation this way:

An extraordinary amount of license is granted to slaves . . . where a blow is illegal, and a slave will not step aside to let you pass him on the street. . . . The Athenian people is not better clothed than the slave or the alien, nor in personal appearance is there any superiority. . . . Slaves in Athens are allowed to indulge in luxury, and indeed in some cases to live magnificently. . . . We have established an equality between our slaves and free men.

Servant boys (here pouring drinks at a Roman orgy) could become free men—and even wealthy slave owners themselves. (From Food and Drink: A Pictorial Archive from Nineteenth-Century Sources, *by Jim Harter, Dover, 1980)*

Most of the newly rich slaves were artisans who were allowed to work with their masters, or on their own, retaining part of their earnings for themselves. That opportunity was not open to household servants, but the changing attitudes affected them, too, in Roman times. Masters began offering household servants modest pay and bonuses; this allowed them to gradually build up sufficient funds so they could buy their freedom. Many former slaves set themselves up in business, buying slaves of their own, and some became extremely rich.

Certainly many who remained slave-servants had an extremely difficult life. That is indicated by some of the laws passed to protect them. In 83 A.D. the Romans passed a law forbidding owners to castrate their slaves. Another forbade masters to sell their slaves into prostitution or into gladiatorial combat. On rare occasions, household servants would band together to attack their master. Some took refuge in religious sanctuaries, as Greek slaves had also been able to do; others fled to become *robbers* on the great highways of the empire.

Still, the movement toward freeing slaves continued. Many household servants became personal companions and valued private advisors; this is not surprising, since many of them were well-educated Greeks. If prized servants like these were ill, their masters might send them abroad to a health resort. Increasingly it became "the thing to do" in Rome to free one's slaves—no doubt this was easier because new supplies were always available. The movement became so popular that laws were even passed regulating the number or proportion of an estate's slaves an owner could free. The laws also specified that only owners above the age of 18 could free slaves and that no slaves over the age of 30 could be freed outright—though they could still buy their freedom.

Servants in these times carried out the whole range of activities involved in running a household or an estate, from dressing hair and cooking food to emptying chamber pots and rubbing down horses, to handling correspondence and keeping household accounts. Some servants entered freely into domestic service in return for the protection and safety that aristocrats or rulers could offer them, or sometimes for the patronage that would permit them to pursue careers as *artists* or *writers*. Many foreigners did so in order to eventually earn citizenship in desirable cities or states.

Housewives during the time of Imperial Rome had considerable freedom and liberty, if they managed upper-class estates, complete with staffs of slaves. If they operated households without such luxuries, though, their lot remained—as ever—closely akin to that of slaves and domestic servants. They were in charge of the raising and tutoring of their children, the cleaning of the house, the tending to the fields and care of livestock, the cooking of family meals, and the manufacture of household items, such as soap, bread, cloth, shoes, and finished clothing. They hauled water from the river for use in the home, washed laundry in the same river, and walked for miles burdened with a heavy cargo of supplies from market or sometimes surplus produce or manufactured goods from their own homes and fields, to be sold at market. The training of future housewives usually began early in childhood and did not terminate until the young teenage girl was finally married and set up in her occupation. Upper-class girls were taught the graces of social life and methods of managing household servants more than the actual labor of housekeeping.

This world came to an abrupt end with the fall of the Western Roman Empire. Neither masters nor servants had much comfort in the centuries that followed in Europe. In the Eastern Roman Empire, slave-servants were in this period drawn primarily from among the Slavs of Eastern Europe. So many of these unfortunate people were brought into servitude in Europe that their name gave us the word *slave*. Slaves did continue to be used to a modest extent in Western Europe, notably on church-owned estates, as would be true for many centuries. The use of slaves declined in the 13th century. However, after the Black Death killed perhaps one-third of Europe's population in the 14th century, slaves were once again eagerly sought, especially in the former Roman lands along the Mediterranean.

In northern and western Europe, domestic laborers tended not to be slaves but servants. They had little personal freedom, however. The fragmented order of medieval Europe and the interlocking nature of its social obligations tied most people to small fiefdoms belonging to petty lords. These employers hired their staff from among the local population, with some being permanent staff and others temporary, employed only while the family was in residence at its estate and let go when the family traveled elsewhere for business or pleasure. In this period, when all society seemed to be fitting itself into a hierarchy, the household servants, too, became ranked in order by responsibility:

First in rank was the steward (*seneschal*). Originally the person in charge of the great hall that was the center of any estate, the steward gradually came to be in charge of all other servants and workers on the estate, inside and out. Later, especially on large properties, the staffs became so large that the job was divided in two, with one steward handling the working of the estate lands and the other supervising the running of the household.

In castles large enough to have a private chapel, this was placed under the supervision of the *chaplain* or *chancellor*, who also came to handle many of the secretarial duties, sometimes supervising household *clerks* or *scribes*. Commonly an integral part of the main building, the chapel was often two stories tall; the upper story, adjoining the owner's private apartments, was for the family, while servants worshipped on the lower floor.

The *chamberlain* had charge of the family's private chambers, while the *wardrobe keeper* handled the family's clothing. Personal servants not only had access to private quarters, they even slept there on rough cots or beds to be on call when needed. As the staff grew larger and more complex, the chamberlain or wardrobe keeper often took on the handling of accounts, reporting to the steward.

Lesser servants had charge of other parts of the house. The *cook*, of course, was supreme in the kitchen. The *butler (bouteillier)* was in charge of the liquid refreshments, stored in bottles, from which the title is drawn. The later rise in standing of the butler may reflect the importance placed on the wines and other beverages in his charge. The *pantler* was overseer of the pantry, where the bread was stored. The *marshal* was head of the stables, supervising the *grooms* and general *stablehands*. All of these servants reported directly to the steward, who supervised each delivery, whether meat, wine, or bread, to be sure that the proper amount and quality were received.

Servants generally slept where they would be most useful. Those who worked in the stables or kitchen area would often sleep there. Male servants would often sleep near the door, (where the *usher* was in charge) or in towers, where they acted partly as *guards*, backing up the *knights* and *squires* who were generally part of the household staff.

The senior servants had considerable recognition. Stewards, often themselves knights, were often well paid and richly dressed. The status of the senior servants is

Household servants, like the cook, footman, housemaid, and page shown here, were often dressed formally for public show. (Authors' archives, 1847)

indicated by the fact that, in later times, titles such as *chancellor* or *chamberlain* would be among the highest in the royal household. And although the pantler, butler, or wardrobe keeper had somewhat less status, still they supervised staffs of their own and had the power to order goods and services from workers such as *tailors*, *launderers*, *bakers*, and *brewers*. (Some large estates even employed a full-time *alewife*, to brew beer, which was the servants' main drink.)

Meanwhile, in other parts of the world, most household servants continued to be slaves. Many of these were, as of old, born slaves or war captives, but after the rise of Islam, the Moslems began a large-scale slave trade. They brought massive numbers of Black Africans across the Sahara to North Africa, with many dying on the terrible desert crossing. Many others were taken eastward to the many Moslem ports on the east coast of Africa, from there to be shipped throughout the Islamic world. Of those who survived the initial journey, many males died during the rough castration required of all—Black or White—designated as household servants. In the Islamic world, many of these castrated males, called *eunuchs*, were assigned to guard the harems of their masters, where the wives and concubines of the house were kept in seclusion. In India, where women were somewhat less secluded and castration was not common, harems were more often guarded by old men or armed female servants. Eunuchs were important in Chinese society; many of those who served in royal or noble households came to have considerable power, much like stewards and chamberlains in Europe. In some periods eunuchs even effectively controlled the country, ruling for their idle masters. Peoples from the lower classes and castes generally filled out the balance of the household laboring staff in these parts of the world.

In Europe, the feudal pattern of household staffing continued for many centuries. But as the modern world,

House servants of various categories were often employed to wait on table as well, like these kneeling to serve meat on spits. (Authors' archives)

with its city-based settlements, began to emerge, there was a new demand for domestic servants. The economic climate was changing rapidly, with increased trade swelling the ranks of the middle-class burghers, who eagerly copied aristocrats in their use of servants. In the 15th and 16th centuries the Portuguese followed the Arab lead in exploiting Africa for cheap labor. The capture and supply of slaves—called *slave running*—formed a lucrative business for several centuries. *Slave runners* supplied Western Europe first, and the American colonies later, with a ready supply of forced workers. Most of these slaves were put to work in the fields, however, and formed significant portions of the domestic labor force only on the plantations of the American South.

In most of Europe, servants were generally not slaves, but wage earners—or hangers-on, who were put up and fed, but otherwise uncompensated for their labor. Country farmers and city merchants, as well as nobles and royalty, employed large numbers of domestic

In India, servants of both colonials and the native rulers were generally drawn from a permanent underclass. (From Food and Drink: A Pictorial Archive from Nineteenth-Century Sources, *by Jim Harter, Dover, 1980)*

servants. The chief supervisor of the domestic laborers was the lady of the house, who managed servants rather than doing the work herself. (Of course, most housewives still did their own housekeeping—generally the same type of work that had been done in field and kitchen since ancient times.)

With the rise of the middle class in the 16th through 18th centuries, servants were increasingly hired to do the housekeeping, cooking, laundry, and child-rearing. Although the vast majority of servant-supported households retained only one general *housemaid* to handle most of these chores, a great many others had virtual armies of servants with countless titles and specializations. In the 18th century, British author Jonathan Swift wrote in his satirical *Directions to Servants* separate chapters for each of the following specialties: the *butler*, the *cook*, the *footman*, the *coachman*, the *groom*, the *house steward* and *land steward*, the *porter*, the *chambermaid*, the *waiting-maid*, the *dairy-maid*, the *children's maid*, the *nurse*, the *laundress*, the *housekeeper*, and the *tutoress*, or *governess*.

The treatment and management of household servants was a matter of considerable concern to masters and to their wives, who frequently handled payment and discipline for them. The lady of the estate or townhouse was responsible for finding honest, capable servants. She was expected to spend money wisely and yet, at the same time, ensure the smooth running of a household that was expected to be as ostentatious as possible.

Seventeenth-century France during the reign of Louis XIV was well known as a courtly society featuring lavish estates staffed by scores of servants. French towns teemed with *lackeys*; these were servants paid only occasionally, if at all, and solely at the discretion of the master, rather than receiving regular wages. They were widely observed to "hang loose upon the town" and create mischief and chaos when not working or assigned to a household. Servants of the time were often considered as members of the family in every sense, and aristocrats sometimes treated them with all the chivalry and politeness that characterized 17th-century French manners. The Duc de Coislin was once so upset at having been tricked into taking the coach seat of two maids that he had to be forcibly restrained from jumping out of the window to offer his gracious apologies to the fair young ladies. Even the *Grand Monarque* Louis XIV was known to have humbly tipped his hat not only to his female servants, but to the *charwomen*, too, as they did the heavy scrub work about the royal court. Servants were so much a part of the distinguished families for which they worked that they occasionally married into them—though surely not without protest from the family. One of the footmen of the Duc de La Rochefoucauld was also his brother-in-law through marriage.

Of course, being part of the family was not all cheery. Servants were usually thought of as children, and their masters as parents. For that reason, servants were frequently beaten, kicked, and verbally abused for their errors and shortcomings, just as the children were. But that did not mean that servants—again like children—could not "sass back" and get visibly indignant or downright angered. Princesse d'Harcourt thought little of hitting her maids, until one recently arrived country girl—fresh from country labor and manners—retaliated and beat the daylights out of her mistress. The girl was not only kept on as a servant, but better respected for having stood up to such a bully. Some household servants—as throughout history—were subject to sexual abuse. Many, notably in England, also lost their given names, being assigned "house names" instead.

The Abbé de Fleury, writing on the subject in the early 18th century, criticized the masters and mistresses of the day. He charged that by retaining as many servants as they possibly could ("Costly the habit as thy purse can buy" was the popular saying), they were concerned not with providing jobs and charity for the poor (as they

While doing the cleaning and polishing, household servants could generally find the time for a little personal byplay. (From Masterpieces in German Art)

pretended), but with imitating grand courtiers and putting on stately and aristocratic airs.

Abbé de Fleury recommended that masters should, according to Christian virtue and French chivalry, "raise" their servants as well as they might if they were their own children. They should provide servants with educational tutoring and religious training; see that they had books and attended mass daily; separate *maids* and *manservants* at the dinner table and in rooming quarters; go out of their way to see that servants got properly married before they could be tempted by sin; set up a "sick room" for those who were ill; provide a lifetime home to those too sickly or old to provide further service; and help set up in business those who took initiatives in that direction. Of course not all French masters were so caring, but some, at least, strove in that direction.

In return for the master's and mistress's kindness, guidance, and protection, the servants also had obligations. The most important seemed to be related to outward appearance, since it was that which most impressed visitors and friends. Drunkenness was probably the most abhorrent offense in a servant, followed by slovenly dress, uncomely grooming, and unpleasant body odor. Servants were to be courteous, of course, as Jonathan Swift admonished the chambermaid: "Do not carry down the necessary vessels (chamber pots) for the fellows to see, but empty them out of the window, for your lady's credit." However, many servants were not punished for rudeness, because they often had a great deal of inside information about a household. Masters and mistresses preferred to put up with some amount of insolence rather than have their servants spread gossip about them around town. Swift—with tongue in cheek—advised servants that: "When you have done a fault, be always pert and insolent, and behave yourself as if you were the injured person; this will immediately put your master, or lady off their mettle."

As for the importance of information learned about householders that might someday be helpful to know (either for blackmail or insight), Swift told the footman that: "When your master and lady are talking together in their bed-chamber, and you have some suspicion that you or your fellow-servants are concerned in what they say, listen at the door for the publick good of all the servants . . . ." Of course, other things might be noted purely for amusement, and this is recommended to the chambermaid: "Get your favorite footman to help you in making your lady's bed; and, if you serve a young couple, the footman and you, as you are turning up the bed-cloaths, will make the prettiest observations in the world; which, whispered about, will be very entertaining to the whole family, and get among the neighborhood." The "whole family" refers to the servant clan, not the householders.

Despite the airs of authority that the servant community might assume, they were hired first and foremost to labor, and few masters or ladies would ease up on that basic requirement. Swift remarked in his directions to the footman that: "It is much to be lamented, that gentlemen of our employment have but two hands to carry plates, dishes, bottles, and the like out of the room at meals; and the misfortune is still the greater, because one of those hands is required to open the door, while you are encumbered with your load."

By the middle of the 18th century the master-servant relationship was becoming less paternal and more cold and formal. In England, the beginnings of manufacturing and large capital enterprises were undermining the country-centered lifestyle of Britons. Many more middle-class people were pushing into crowded cities with rows of townhouses. Servants employed there had more opportunities for disgracing themselves and their householders than they had on country estates. They frequented alehouses and brothels and became involved in thievery, gambling, and prostitution while enjoying days off. London, as the commercial center of the world, had more domestic labor than any other city in the world right up into the 20th century. There were quite a number of men employed to work outside houses as *coachmen*, *stablemen*, and *gardeners*, but only *houseboys*, *butlers*, and *footmen* had much to do with the actual housework.

The vast majority of servants were country girls who had left the farm for excitement and fortune, sometimes for education and vocational training. They found what most country girls had been finding for years—that homemaking for one's husband, or as a domestic servant to others, was one of the few professions a woman could enter without losing her reputation. One observer in 1753 remarked that an "amazing number" of women sought housework in London, yet there was always a dire shortage of good help. The growth of cities made the plight of newly arrived peasant girls even worse. They were dropped off in London by the wagon load, and were immediately harassed by *pimps* and *madames* trying to turn them to prostitution. One writer in 1776 offered:

. . . a word of advice to such young women as may arrive strangers in town . . . . Immediately on their arrival . . .

and sometimes sooner, even upon the road to it, there are miscreants of both sexes on the watch to seduce the fresh country maiden, with infinite protestations of friendship, service, love and pity, to prostitution . . . . For this reason, the very carriages which convey them are hunted and examined; fernal hirelings who . . . put on the demure shew of modesty and sanctity for their deception. If she applies to an office of intelligence, 'tis odds but she falls into the hands of some procuress . . . .

Wagons were usually met by mistresses seeking servants, and they frequently sought the youngest and most innocent girls, believing them to be most malleable, least troublesome, and possessed of the smallest appetites. Orphan girls farmed out from charity schools were usually picked up by poor and lower-class families, who kept them on as *drudges* for room and board. Although orphan girls had been trained in the "art of housewifery" from infancy and were bound to a mandatory four-year tour of duty after being released from the charity school, they were still unwanted by most fine householders, who found "their depravity truly deplorable" and their bodily infirmities often too considerable to tolerate. Social reformers deplored this "most ruinous practice" of hiring out orphans, and investigators admitted finding that "some of these poor girls had been seduced by their masters, that some had run away . . and that the health of the others, not good when they left the school, had been completely ruined by ill usage."

Most servants were young girls who either left the service when it was time for them to marry and become housewives in their own right, or were spinsters who held their positions as long as they could. Older spinsters were at some disadvantage for several reasons: For one, they demanded higher wages for their long years of service. They were also apt to slow down in their enthusiasm and desire to please, if not in their physical abilities.

In addition, they were not sexually desired by either the master or his sons (young maids who were could be excused for many faults in return for sexual favors). Finally, they were generally thought less appropriate for such work than young girls. Once the more experienced, and therefore costly, maids were sent away from a household, they were forced "to go into lodgings and there subsist on their little savings, till they get places agreeable to their inclinations . . . and this is one of the grand sources which furnish this town with prostitutes," as John Fielding wrote about London in 1753.

Most young girls did not wait to get old in their jobs, but married as soon as the opportunity arose. They then joined the ranks of housewives and often worked much harder in that vocation than they ever had as servants. Since they were lower-class people for the most part, they generally married into situations in which they had to help their laboring husbands. Toward this end, they turned to peddling goods in the streets, taking in wash and needlework, or wet nursing. All this work was in addition to housecleaning and cooking, of course, and manufacturing goods for home use.

Housewives living in town—especially those married to *shopkeepers* and *merchants*—fared better. They usually had fewer things to manufacture at home, had no field work, and frequently had at least one maid to help handle the keeping of the house. The wives of successful merchants often worked mostly in their husbands' businesses, while at the same time being responsible for the management of their own household labor staff. If merchants or shopkeepers were not so prosperous, their wives would often work at the shop or warehouse, in addition to doing a large share of the housework and cooking.

In the 19th century there was a great rise in the use of domestic servants, particularly in England and the United States, where standards of living and the number of middle-class households were rising sharply with the industrialization of society. With factory work open to men, their ranks among domestic labor shrank considerably, until only the richest families retained a butler. Girls, meanwhile, were less needed for farm work, which was becoming increasingly mechanized. They had few alternatives to becoming servants. In fact, most lower- and middle-class people preferred sending their daughters to fine families for proper training in good manners and morals, while they were waiting to be married. By the end of the 19th century, one out of five British households employed domestic servants, and an estimated one out of three girls between the ages of 15 and 20 were so situated.

Servants were treated much more indifferently during the Victorian age than they had been in earlier times. No longer part of the family, they were only workers, who were expected to be as invisible and silent as possible. The striking of servants was made illegal in England in the 1860's. At about the same time, girl servants were allowed to sleep in attics, instead of in kitchens or in under-stairway bins as they had been earlier. Men servants still slept downstairs, to protect against burglars. Despite these gains in working conditions, servants were no longer treated as warmly or unselfishly as they often had been in the past. They were seldom educated by their masters and at the first sign of illness or impudence were readily sent packing penniless and *short*—that is, without adequate references for finding another situation. Unemployed servants frequently resorted to registry offices to find work, but these agencies often turned out to be nothing more than fronts for brothels.

Those girls who remained on the job were often forced to provide sexual favors for masters and their sons; and some—known as *dolly-mops*—did the same with visitors, shopkeepers, and just about anyone else who might be in a position to help a poor servant girl. A great many servant girls began their service before they even reached their tenth birthdays, and by the time they were 20 suffered from chronic digestive and nervous disorders accompanied by anemia caused by a lack of fresh air and long, monotonous work days. There were very few times when they were allowed to leave the homes where they worked. When they did they were looked out for by "friendly societies" of volunteer ladies, who formed to oversee the moral direction of this large laboring class, mostly children and young women, who were no longer being properly "raised" by the householders employing them.

In the United States, servants had typically been Black African slaves in the plantation societies of the South, where their numbers were greatest. In the North, while many people had hired servants, the occupation was never nearly as important as it was in England. In Victorian England, butlers wore elegant black suits with coat-tails, while the head *housekeeper* wore a black silk dress to distinguish her from the uniformed chambermaids and *service-maids*. American servants had no such sharp hierarchical structure, and they all usually did whatever kind of work was most necessary at a given moment. Of course, even in England, the countless titles allotted servants were often just for pomp and show. Many a chambermaid served dinner; many a service-maid helped the cook, laundress, or nursery maid in their routine chores; and many a housemaid complained bitterly at being put to work in the stables.

After the Civil War in the United States, freed Black slaves became paid domestic servants. In 1870 half of all the women earning wages did so through domestic labor. By 1910 some 7 percent of the entire national labor force were domestics, representing as many as two million laborers, 90 percent of whom were women.

Shortly after World War I, however, industry opened up new opportunities for women seeking to earn wages. Many left domestic work, preferring the personal freedom of living in their own quarters and doing what they wished during their off-work hours. Others sought a greater chance of promotion, which was virtually impossible in domestic service. A lady who had served for many years generally became simply an "old maid." Except for the housekeeper, all of the higher paid jobs, like cooking and supervising, were usually given to men.

Chambermaids with excellent hairdressing skills were much prized by ladies of fashion. (By Aubrey Beardsley, from Collected Drawings)

This was especially true in Europe, where *chefs* and butlers were held in quite high esteem. American women had largely abandoned servant work by the early 20th century, leaving it largely to European immigrants and Blacks, many of whom emigrated into northern urban areas. On the West Coast menservants became even more numerous than women-servants—a rare occurrence in the history of the occupation—owing to the large influx of Chinese and other East Asian men seeking such work in a region where few European immigrants and Blacks were available for it.

By the end of World War II, servants in both America and Europe were to be found only in rather wealthy households. Child labor laws and the establishment of universal education undermined the availability of cheap child labor. More important, mechanization and the rise

of consumerism transformed the modern household. Refrigerators, washing and drying machines, vacuum cleaners, stoves, sewing machines, and all the other household gadgets that flooded the market from the 1920's on, made housekeeping less of a chore than before. Packaged foods, soap, manufactured clothes, and shoes made obsolete much of the work traditionally done by servants. The automobile did away with stables and horse-keeping, and for the most part made it unnecessary to retain a *driver* or *chauffeur*. In addition, a family's extra money was more likely to be spent on these new products—cars, washing machines, radios, and televisions—than on hiring servants. Housework became more manageable, and most middle-class families dropped their servants and left all the work to the traditional homemaker—the housewife.

Though freed from formal servitude, these dispirited Black women remain trapped as servants. (National Archives, Bureau of Agricultural Economics, 83-FB-272, 1899)

Housewives had always done the domestic labor in lower-class homes, but now they would be left to do it in most households. Servants are still employed today, but for the most part, only by wealthy families. After the 1940's most housewives received help only in the person of the *day cleaner*, the *char-woman*, or the *one-day-a-week lady*. These cleaners—mostly women, but sometimes men—help with the heavy cleaning, and sometimes the laundry and ironing. They are paid for their day's work, after which they return to their own homes and families; the next day they do the same for another household. Otherwise, the manual labor of housekeeping, as well as the cooking, child care, gardening, errand-running, and so on have traditionally been heaped onto the housewife.

Recently, it has become more fashionable for men to share—or more often to "help out with"—these chores. Occasionally, when women work outside the home and their husbands do not, these *househusbands* assume the majority of the housekeeping chores. For the most part, though, the bulk of the domestic labor is still the responsibility of the housewife. Aided by modern gadgets and machines, to be sure, housewives still spend countless hours working in isolation, doing monotonous work without pay or professional recognition. They either forego a professional career or manage with difficulty to have both a career and virtually all the household responsibilities as well. This is true not only in the Western world but also in many socialist and communist countries supposedly built on equality for all.

Some women's groups are now advocating pay and professional recognition for women's roles as *household managers* or *domestic engineers*. Certainly not all women despise their lots, nor are all men thrilled to devote their lives to the business or work world. But both lack effective freedom of choice in a world where such roles remain overwhelmingly determined by gender.

Few contemporary households retain servants in the traditional manner. In May of 1981, for example, the number of butlers in Britain was reported to have fallen to 98, compared with some 30,000 just before World War II. Just 10 British households (excluding royal houses) retained the traditional staff of servants—footman, personal maid, housekeeper, cook, and nanny—while only 30 had a butler, housekeeper, and maid. In North America the economy is stronger and more people can afford live-in help. But servants are widely employed today only in those countries that have a considerable population of affluent householders and a large, pitifully cheap labor pool, capable of being exploited much as slaves once were in the American South.

Few private homes today employ full-time butlers, but some butlers provide their services on a free-lance basis for special occasions. (By Arthur Rothstein, from The Depression Years, *Dover, 1978)*

The most notable example of this situation today is South Africa, where rich mineral resources (especially diamonds) have attracted many White Europeans; they control the wealth, depriving Black natives of economic and political rights, and employing them at sub-poverty wage levels as domestics. The *New York Times* reported on March 30, 1981, that some of the 800,000 Black domestics employed in South Africa were beginning to form the South African Domestic Workers Association, hoping to raise their standard of living. In a country where $60 a week is considered poverty level, most domestic laborers earn only $9 to $13 in the country, up to $20 in the suburbs, and only very rarely above $30—all this for work-weeks of up to 70 hours.

In addition, most of the Black live-in domestics are women who are the sole support of their children; but they are forbidden by racist laws to have either their children or their husbands live with them in the White homes. They must resort, instead, to leaving their families behind in distant "homelands," visiting them only occasionally. The White householders are generally irate at the unionization attempts, and one mistress angrily complained to Leah Tutu, the director of the Race Relations Institutes Project on Domestic Workers: "Who do you think you are, giving these pro-union pamphlets to my girls?" Mrs. Tutu responded: "We don't give pamphlets to girls. We give them to women."

Human nature being what it is, however, as long as inequalities exist between sexes, races, and classes, some people will continue to be employed—and exploited—by others to perform daily household chores.

For related occupations in this volume, *Helpers and Aides*, see the following:

Child Nurses
Drivers
Launderers
Movers

Sanitation Workers
Social Workers

For related occupations in other volumes of the series, see
the following:
  in *Artists and Artisans*:
  Painters
  Sculptors
in *Clothiers*:
  Tailors and Dressmakers
in *Communicators*:
  Authors
  Clerks
  Scribes
in *Financiers and Traders*:
  Stewards and Supervisors
in *Harvesters*:
  Farmers
  Gardeners
in *Leaders and Lawyers*:
  Political Leaders
in *Restaurateurs and Innkeepers* (forthcoming):
  Brewers
  Cooks
  Dairy Operators
in *Scholars and Priests* (forthcoming):
  Teachers
in *Warriors and Adventurers* (forthcoming):
  Prostitutes

Social Workers

Social work as a profession emerged only in the late 19th century, although its roots reach back to much earlier times. While individual and local charitable activities are as old as humanity, organized social relief did not appear until late Roman times, when the early Christian order of the *Deaconesses* began to bring aid directly into the slum quarters of the time. The Deaconesses were mostly wealthy Roman matrons who, in accordance with ideas of Christian charity, visited the homes of the sick and the needy, distributing food, clothing, and medicine. In doing so, they apparently originated the ideas of *friendly visiting*, as these services later came to be called, and of working on a district plan. The Deaconess order died out in the fifth and sixth centuries A.D., however, and their model was not followed elsewhere for many centuries.

Charitable actions in Europe, as well as in India and the Islamic world, came to be focused more on caring for the poor in hospitals, than on bringing aid into the poor communities. The early Christian hospitals, indeed, were not primarily medical institutions, but were intended to give shelter to the poor, the orphaned, the homeless, and the traveler, as well as to the sick. The people who staffed these hospitals were not social workers but members of religious orders who gradually came to specialize in medical work. With the Reformation, and the resulting suppression of many monasteries and abbeys, especially in Northern Europe, even that avenue of aid was cut off. The state did not move to fill the gap for many centuries. It was left to local parishes to handle the problems of the poor in their communities, under such acts as the English Poor Law and its counterparts in America and elsewhere. The result was an ineffectual, haphazard, often cruel system of poorhouses and workhouses. The aged and sick—those who could not care for themselves—were put together in institutions called poorhouses. Later, workhouses were established where the able-bodied homeless poor could earn their keep. But often these institutions exploited the poor and helpless. The poor and orphaned were often *indentured*—that is, virtually sold to do work for a specified number of months or years.

In the 17th century, a French parish priest, Vincent de Paul, developed an organized plan for alleviating and eliminating poverty. Like the Deaconesses of a thousand years earlier, he proposed systematic visiting of the poor. His plan was to provide not only food and clothing, but also continuous constructive aid, including skills training. Some of his *friendly visitors* recognized the need for social services in connection with the hospitals, to supplement the services of overworked nursing nuns and to follow up on released patients. To meet this need, St. Vincent established the Sisters of Charity, who became the first medical social workers. St. Vincent's ideas were first put into practice only in medical areas, but introduced the concept of organized social work to modern Europe.

With industrialization and rapid urban growth, social ills grew faster than a disorganized assortment of local relief societies could deal with them, and in the early part of the 19th century, the idea of systematic social service was beginning to spread. In the 1820's, a Scottish clergyman, Thomas Chalmers, set up friendly visiting in Glasgow on a district plan, with each district under charge of a *deacon*. This program stressed frugal habits and character reformation, more than the distribution of money, food, and other financial assistance. In 1843 the Association for Improving Conditions of the Poor (AICP) was formed in New York to coordinate the various charities of the city; each political ward had an advisory committee to provide relief and friendly visitors.

The AICP served as a model for other general relief societies, both in North America and Europe. The German city of Elberfeld even instituted conferences among its friendly visitors, perhaps the earliest *case conferences* in social work. In these early groups, men—especially clergymen, aristocrats, or professionals—usually organized and administered the relief programs. But virtually all of the actual *charity workers* were women volunteers, married or single women of religious leanings and good families, many of them influential members of their communities. The image of the early charity worker was very much that of "Lady Bountiful," dispensing largesse to the poor.

In the last third of the 19th century, that image began to change, with the founding of the Charity Organization Society (originally called the Society for Organising Charitable Relief and Repressing Mendicity) in London in 1869. The COS established the principle of investigating conditions of the poor and providing relief on the basis of assessed needs. The many Charity Organization Societies that sprang up in Europe and America focused less on giving charity and more on changing the life patterns of the poor, through moral influence and training. Great stress was placed on distinguishing between the "deserving poor" and the "undeserving poor," since charity had been accused of simply perpetuating the problems of the latter. These investigative procedures required larger, more permanent staffs than previous charitable efforts had, and by 1881 the COS found that it had too few volunteers to carry out its inquiries.

As a result, the COS established the first distinct group of paid *social workers*. At the start, these were mostly young men—called *collectors*, *enquirers*, or *inquiry agents*—who were hired to obtain and confirm information about individual cases. However, gradually more women, who would formerly have worked as unpaid volunteers, turned to social work as one of the few salaried occupations open to "respectable" women at the time. Early male charity workers tended to be from the lower middle classes and relied on their salary for living expenses. Their female counterparts—paid and unpaid—tended to be of higher social status. Many of the women were wives or daughters of business, professional, or clerical men. For these women, a salary was a move toward independence, but was not their sole source of support.

Although most early social workers were concerned with individual casework, some took a different approach. Samuel Barnett, a parish priest in the London community of Whitechapel, put the case this way: "The poor need more than food: they need the knowledge, the character, the happiness which is the Gift of God to this age." Barnett proposed to establish educational and cultural centers right in the poor communities, and in 1884—along with his wife, herself an experienced social worker, and some university students—he founded Toynbee Hall. This was the first *settlement house*, so-called because the social workers actually settled in the community.

Social reformers from North America came to visit Barnett and carried his ideas back home. Among them

The very picture of an early social worker, Evangeline Booth, dubbed "The White Angel of the Slums," poses with two "street urchins" she is sheltering with the Salvation Army, founded by her father. (Library of Congress, 1907)

were Stanton Coit, who in 1886 returned to the United States to establish the Neighborhood Guild, later called the University Settlement, on New York's Lower East Side; and Jane Addams, who founded Chicago's famous Hull House in 1889.

By Barnett's death in 1913, over 400 settlement houses were active in the United States alone, and the movement had spread through Western Europe, North America, and Southeast Asia. Although many of the early settlement workers, like the Barnetts, had independent means and could work without pay, this movement established community work as a prime and increasingly important area of social service, one that soon required training and paid salaries.

Police officers brought orphaned or abandoned children to New York City's Commissioners of Charity, who provided some housing and training. (By Paul Frenzeny, from Harper's Weekly, January 30, 1869)

Some early settlement houses were segregated by sex, with the staff similarly segregated. Samuel Barnett's original idea had been for male settlement houses, but his wife began to found women's settlement houses as well. Male *settlers* generally proved more interested in the organizational and administrative side of social work, while women were usually more concerned with direct contact. Women's settlement houses established a wider sphere of activities, setting the pattern for modern community social work, much of which is not segregated by sex.

In the process, women also created for themselves a whole range of new careers in social work, and came to be influential in social work training, while men more often played administrative or honorary committee roles. Many early social workers were, again like the Barnetts, married couples doing complementary work, often divided by sex roles. Women worked in areas that focused on personal contact, especially relating to women, children, and the home, being thought more suitable than men to deal with domestic matters. Men dealt with adult men and delinquent boys, and were more often appointed to be *inspectors* or to fill other positions of authority, although a woman might often move into a supervisory or administrative position on the death of her husband-partner.

A developing body of theory and technique—resulting in what its practitioners called a scientific approach to charity—required some methods of training for social workers. As early as 1873 the British reformer Octavia Hill established lecture and training programs for charity and settlement workers. Gradually demand grew for trained people to work in and run the charity organizations. Nathaniel S. Rosenau, of the Buffalo (New York) Charity Organization Society, for example, thought that charitable societies should not be run by "superannuated clergymen" or "political favorites" but by people "who are specially trained, who have a calling for the work, and who mean to devote themselves to it." In 1898, adopting a proposal by American charity worker Mary Richmond, the New York City Charity Organization Society opened a summer school, providing the first formal education in social work; by 1904 this had become the Columbia University School of Social Work. The first full-fledged social work school was founded in Amsterdam in 1899. This was soon followed by others in England, America, elsewhere in Europe, and by 1920 in Latin America, starting with a school in Santiago, Chile. In these decades charity and settlement workers shaped themselves into a professional group who called themselves *social workers*.

The 20th century brought two major changes in the thrust of social work. First, with the rise of psychology in the early part of the century, social workers began to think of themselves not just as friendly visitors but as social physicians, analyzing and helping to solve the problems of their clients. The social worker's focus was no longer simply on relieving socio-economic problems, but on easing the "adjustment" of anyone who was troubled, including many people—soldiers and civilians—whose lives were disrupted by World War I. The result was that, for the first time, social casework moved "above the poverty line." This tendency accelerated with a second major change: national governments, especially those in the industrialized countries, began to assume responsibility for various aspects of social welfare, starting with the development of governmental programs like the Social Security Act in the United States in the 1930's. The social worker's potential "clientele" therefore expanded in many countries to include virtually every citizen.

With the need for large staffs to run national social service programs, social work became one of the fastest-

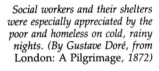

Social workers and their shelters were especially appreciated by the poor and homeless on cold, rainy nights. (By Gustave Doré, from London: A Pilgrimage, *1872)*

growing professions in the 20th century, with the demand for professionally trained social workers far outstripping the supply. Because of the continuing shortage, many social workers, even today, are employed with only a college degree, but no specialized training, while others have some special training but no degree. Many have little incentive to become professionally trained, partly because salaries for social workers have always been relatively low. Many early social workers had independent incomes and required no salaries, certainly not substantial ones, while for the vast army of volunteers, social work was supposed to be its own reward. As a result, social workers—often single women, thought by society to be making up for the lack of a family of their own—have had limited success in reaching salary parity with other professionals.

Incentives for training have also been lacking for professional reasons. Advancement opportunities are limited. Social workers with graduate degrees, such as a master's degree in social work (M.S.W.) or a doctorate, generally move into the few supervisory or administrative positions. Other social workers remain in positions at or near entry level in understaffed offices, spending much of their time in routine work that could be done by people with neither a college degree nor special training. A related problem is that social work, as a profession, does not have a clear identity but is a field encompassing a wide variety of activities. For example, the range of groups combining in 1936 to form the British Federation of Social Workers included *family caseworkers, occupational therapists, public health officers, probation officers, psychiatric social workers, tuberculosis care committee secretaries, women housing managers*, and *moral welfare workers*. The increase in governmental social work since then has only expanded the range of social work activities. As a result, social workers have had some difficulty in defining their roles and setting professional standards, and social work itself has had less status and attraction than related professions, such as medicine.

Some social work specialties have, however, established themselves in the 20th century. *Family and child welfare workers* are the successors of the 19th-century traditional charity workers. Today, in addition to providing financial aid and skills training, these workers are also involved in marriage and maternal counseling, home and family education, home-help programs for the elderly or for families that might otherwise be broken up, family planning, and a wide variety of protective services for orphaned or ill-treated children and unwed mothers.

The emphases of family and child welfare programs vary widely among the countries of the world. Great Britain and the Scandinavian countries, for example, have far more extensive home-care services than the United States does. The United States and Western Europe have active marriage counseling services, while the Soviet Union has almost none. And many countries—except predominantly Catholic ones—put great emphasis on family planning.

Some social workers have come to specialize in *youth welfare work*, as leaders and counselors in the wide variety of youth groups in various countries. Some of these counselors work with government-affiliated groups, like Sweden's "leisure-time" groups for young people or the Soviet Union's government-sponsored youth groups. Other youth welfare workers are affiliated with religious groups like the YMCA or the Salvation Army. Still others are part of independent, voluntary groups like the Boy Scouts. While most family and child welfare workers have traditionally been women, youth welfare workers have often been segregated, with men and women working with youths of their own sex.

From Samuel Barnett's original *settlers* developed a large group of *community social workers*. The early settlement workers were extremely important in easing the adjustment of millions of immigrants into new lives in strange lands, especially in the United States. Such workers have applied similar experience and skills to dealing with the problems of refugees and displaced persons throughout the century. Originally, settlement workers emphasized the rapid assimilation of immigrants, encouraging them to give up much of their previous culture. In recent decades, however, social workers have encouraged the retention and appreciation of the immigrant's ethnic heritage.

Community social workers also provide services for handicapped people, military veterans, and victims of disasters, working in connection with public and private organizations like the International Red Cross. Because many of the early community workers were social reformers, they used the educational and cultural facilities of the settlement houses and community centers to help formulate and spread ideas that later were enacted into legislation, such as workers' compensation, child labor laws, establishment of juvenile courts, and provision of pensions for mothers. Community social workers continue that shaping role today in rural areas

Some social workers cared for all living creatures; here Henry Bergh, founder of the Society for the Prevention of Cruelty to Animals, inspects exhausted horses pulling an overloaded streetcar. (By Sol Eytinge, Jr., from Harper's Weekly, *September 21, 1872)*

and in developing countries, often in groups with religious affiliations, such as Quaker or Catholic relief societies, or with international connections, such as with the United Nations.

Medical social workers, in Great Britain called *almoners*, are descended from St. Vincent de Paul's early Sisters of Charity. Modern medical social workers act primarily as liaisons between medical personnel and patients, ensuring that physicians know the social factors relating to a patient's illness and that the patient has the proper support during recuperation. Although introduced in the 19th century by Charles Loch, a prime mover in the London Charity Organization Society, hospital almoning has been carried out almost entirely by women, the first being a Miss Stewart appointed to the Royal Free Hospital in London in 1895. In the early years, almoners had to be women of considerable status, tact, and independence, since their services in the hospitals required the permission of the virtually all-male medical staff of the hospitals. From England, the practice spread elsewhere, being introduced in the United States in 1905, at the Massachusetts General Hospital in Boston. In the United States, medical social workers are often drawn from the nursing profession, while in Europe their training is primarily in social work.

A closely related specialty, which sits even more firmly on the borderline between medical work and social work, is that of the *psychiatric social worker*. This specialty developed gradually with the century, especially in the 1920's and 1930's, as the interest in psychological social work—always greater in the United States than in Europe—sparked advanced training in mental health and attachment of these workers to psychiatric hospitals. The first psychiatric social workers were employed by neurological hospital clinics in Boston and New York in 1905. Psychiatric social services have been especially useful during and after wartime periods, and in establishing modern halfway houses—places where released patients can live, mostly independently but with some supervision and guidance, before going completely on their own—and follow-up of mental patients. Some highly trained social workers have also gone into private practice, working as *therapists*. This gives them increased status, pay, and independence.

Probation and parole officers are social workers who work within the prison system. The probation and parole movement was initiated in Birmingham, England, in the 1840's, when M. Davenport Hill instituted a system of reviewing a prisoner's background and current state, before considering the prisoner for release and police supervision. In the 1870's the English Temperance Society appointed *missionaries* to appear in court to counsel people charged with drunkenness. By the 1880's, such groups began to be appointed probation officers by the court, and the practice had spread to the United States, first to Boston. A related specialty was that of *institutional inspector*. Such inspectors were generally appointed by the national government to oversee institutions such as orphanages, reformatories, and workhouses, some of which were carryovers from earlier times. Under the English Poor Law, for example, local authorities appointed inspectors called Poor Law Guardians to supervise workhouses.

Parole and probation officers and institutional inspectors have usually been men, with women generally being appointed only for dealing with women and children. In the 19th century, at least, couples were often appointed jointly to carry out complementary work, with the woman sometimes succeeding to her husband's more senior post on his death. Because this area of social work never had the same amount of aristocratic patronage as did charity work or almoning, probation and parole officers and institutional inspectors have not had as much status as professionals in other areas of social work.

From being dispensers of charity to the poor, social workers have—in only a century—come to be agents of planned social change and counselors to the whole of society.

For related occupations in other volumes of the series, see the following:

in *Healers* (forthcoming):
  Nurses
  Physicians and Surgeons
  Psychologists and Psychiatrists
in *Leaders and Lawyers*:
  Police Officers
  Prison Guards and Executioners
in *Scholars and Priests* (forthcoming):
  Monks and Nuns

Undertakers

Throughout human history, people in most cultures have disposed of their dead without the intervention of specialists. Whether the body was to be buried in the earth, cremated, consigned to the sea, or exposed in the air to be picked clean by birds and animals, the relatives and friends of the dead have generally been responsible for cleaning, anointing, and dressing the body according to the local custom (jobs often delegated to older women); for having the grave dug or the pyre prepared; and for carrying out all the culturally prescribed rituals and ceremonies at and after the person's death (often the special charge of the oldest son or heir of the family).

At some times and places, however, the rituals and practices surrounding death have become so complex and burdensome that specialists have been employed literally to *undertake* them on behalf of the family. The most notable early culture in which this occurred was that of the Egyptians, whose pyramidal monuments to the dead are still the best-known feature of their culture, many thousands of years later. The cult of the dead began in Egypt around 4000 B.C. and continued for thousands of years, until well after the Egyptians had come under foreign domination. Originally bodies were dismembered—as the mythical Osiris, god of the dead, had been. But the practice of mummification, a form of preservation through dehydration and chemical treatment, was soon developed.

In their desire to honor and preserve their dead, the Egyptians built huge *necropolises* (cities of the dead), where bodies were entombed along with rich funeral treasures and where ritual prayers and offerings were made at stated times throughout the year. These necropolises were built generally on the west side of the Nile, in the direction of the setting sun, or on the western outskirts of the city, built away from the living population for sanitary reasons. Because these richly appointed tombs required protection, maintenance, and religious attendance, a group of *priests* acted as *tomb chaplains* for the necropolises, performing religious functions in place of the family of the deceased. These were an ill-regarded class of lesser priests, mistrusted by the general population and often accused of fraud and theft, but it was they who gradually assumed the responsibility of directing virtually all funeral arrangements.

These early priestly *undertakers* (*Kher-hebs*) were called in immediately after a death and supervised the activities of the various funerary specialists. Assistants removed the body and transported it by sledge and then by boat across the river to the necropolis. *Professional mourners* were hired to sing funeral dirges around the city and to accompany the body across the river with wailing laments. After a ritual bath in the purification tent, the body was taken to the embalming tent. This was generally a portable hut. The embalming tents for pharaohs, however, were sometimes permanent structures. There the embalming staff took over.

Embalming was originally for the royal family only, but early became extended to the nobility as a mark of royal favor, called the "pharaoh's gift." Eventually, however, it was extended to all who could afford the procedure, including even peasants and traders. Poor people often had simply a dry burial over beds of charcoal; this provided a cheap sort of natural mummification, allowing dehydration and decomposition without the moist rot that accompanies burial in the earth. More affluent Egyptian families were offered a choice of three types of embalming, and were shown wooden models simulating the results. These varied according to the time and attention given to the procedure and the quality of the materials employed.

The most elaborate and expensive form of embalming involved the removal of the brain and vital organs, which were separately embalmed and preserved in four *canopic jars*. After this the body cavities were washed and filled with spices and resins; then the body was soaked in a soda solution for 40 days, and finally wrapped in a linen shroud, ready for entombment. A less expensive method of embalming dispensed with the evisceration and employed injection of the body cavities with cedar oil, soaking in an alkali solution, and later flushing out of the dissolved soft organs, the result being preserved skin and bones. The third method involved flushing the intestines and soaking the corpse in a soda solution for 70 days; in later practice the corpse was soaked in pitch, or bitumen, the result being a black mummy.

All of these procedures were carried out under the supervision of the head *embalmer*, who wore the mask of a jackal, portraying Anubis, the god credited with reassembling the dismembered Osiris, god and ruler of the dead. The actual work was performed by assistants. Among these was a *dissector* (cutter), who actually disemboweled the body, following the embalmer's directions, and accompanied by the embalmer's recital of

In early Egyptian times, mummies were sometimes brought out to share feasts with the rest of the family. (From Museum of Antiquity, *by L. W. Yaggy and T. L. Haines, 1882)*

appropriate incantations. The *pollinctors* (salters) were a class of *apothecaries* who prepared the oils, spices, and solutions used in the various embalming processes. Sometimes one person performed both functions, along with the final wrapping in linen. The whole process often took two to three months; the bandaging alone took 15 days. The resulting embalmed corpse would generally be placed in a painted and decorated coffin; all liquid and solid waste matter would be bottled and packaged separately for preservation along with the body. The mummy would then be lowered into its final resting place by a complicated system of sledges, winches, and pulleys. In some periods the mummy was returned to the family home, where it occupied a special room, being brought out to take part in various family affairs and sometimes even being used as collateral for a loan.

Embalmers inspired fear and revulsion, along with a little awe, among the general population. The profession was regarded as loathsome and, although lucrative, made embalmers and their families virtual outcasts, reinforcing the tendency toward hereditary practice of the trade. A description of an embalmer form the Sallier

III papyrus reflects the popular view of such a practitioner:

> The embalmer's fingers are evil-smelling, for their odor is that of corpses. His eyes burn with the heat. He is too tired to stand up to his own daughter. He passes the day in cutting garments out of old rags for his clothing is an abomination to him.

Early embalmers were almost always men, but in later periods, female embalmers were sometimes employed to handle female corpses. Embalmers worked under government regulation and protection, moving their portable huts to tomb sites within their assigned geographical area. Surviving records show that embalmers sometimes had sharp disputes regarding jurisdiction over a corpse to be buried near the borderlines.

Embalmers were allowed by law to live among the general population, and were protected from harassment by special laws in some periods. However, most lived in small villages near the necropolises, along with all the other workers who were employed in those cities of the dead, including *police, masons, construction laborers, gardeners, painters, sculptors, carpenters*, and various *shopkeepers* who supplied these workers with the necessities of life. All of these reported to the chief administrator of the necropolis, in Thebes called "the Prince of Western Thebes." He was responsible for the whole bureaucracy, including the receipt of fees for mummification and for the Egyptian version of *perpetual care* for the tombs. In times when Egypt's economy was healthy, as in the 13th century B.C. under Ramses II, all of these workers were well provided for. Each worker's family lived in a separate house; the workers were provided with meat, fish, beer, and fresh fruits and vegetables; and the pharaoh boasted:

> I have had the shops filled for you with all kinds of things ... sandals and apparel so that you may be clothed all the year round and have good shoes on your feet every day.

In the four thousand years of Egyptian history before the Romans conquered the area, around the time of Christ, the Egyptian embalmers are estimated to have mummified more than 500 million bodies and innumerable animals, ranging from cats to crocodiles.

This mass mummification, however, began to be a tremendous burden on the Egyptian population. When mummification became widespread, burial space became scarce, and private tombs were converted into family chambers for dozens or even hundreds of bodies over the years. The cost of embalming every member of the family, of maintaining their tombs, and of paying tomb priests for continual ritual prayer and offerings, became more and more difficult to bear. Also, the oils and chemicals required for the embalming process were more expensive after Egyptians lost ready access to these substances in the centuries before the birth of Christ. As a result, tombs began to fall into disrepair, and tomb priests no longer received regular payments. Embalming became more careless, and embalmers sometimes cavalierly broke or cut off limbs to make a body fit into the available sarcophagus. The huge class of embalmers could no longer be supported in the style to which they had become accustomed; some even went on strike during the reign of Ramses III, in the 11th century B.C., noting that their wages were 18 days overdue, and they were starving. They apparently received some satisfaction from the pharaoh's representatives, for they soon returned to work, but strikes occurred occasionally from that time on.

As Egypt successively passed under the domination of the Persians, the Greeks, and the Romans, the practice of embalming once again came to be reserved for the privileged few. The number of tomb priests and embalmers dwindled, and many of the vast necropolises—built of stone, to last, unlike the flimsy huts that had housed the living—were converted into villages, with many tombs becoming homes. The mass of the Egyptian population, unable to afford embalmers, simply buried their unembalmed, uncoffined dead near holy places—or piled them up inside the temples. The now-poor Egyptian population, both embalmers and general citizens, turned to looting the treasures of the tombs of their ancestors, a practice that has continued—with assistance from Arabs and Europeans—into the 20th century.

People in other cultures, without the cult of the dead that characterized the Egyptians, had much less need for funerary specialists, especially where the dead were cremated, as was often the case in early Greece. There the older women of the family generally washed and anointed the body and watched over it for signs of life during the required three days before actual burial. Funeral arrangements were also generally handled by the family, often being made by the person before his own death. Even so, some professionals existed. *Corpse bearers* would often be hired to carry the body on its bier to the site of cremation or burial. *Professional mourners*, mostly women, were also hired to conduct the watch with the family and to swell the burial procession. These mourners wailed funeral laments and tore at their bodies, portraying the grief of the family; some, notably Carian women, were such zealous professional mourners that the Greek writer Lucian complained that the living at such funerals were in a sorrier state than the dead. Indeed, the mourners were often depicted in Greek art with wildly dishevelled hair and streams of blood trickling from their cheeks and breasts. Later custom and legislation somewhat muted these public and professional displays of grief.

For rich and powerful Greeks, enormously elaborate funeral arrangements were made. Professional singers and musicians were brought in to sing dirges by great poets like Pindar and Simonides. For the cremation of his friend Hephaestus, for example, Alexander the Great built a six-story pyre, with singers performing from inside statues on the corners of the upper stories during the pre-cremation ceremonies. Tales of Greek mythology tell how Andromache herself led the bards and the wailing women in their laments at the funeral of her husband, Hector. So much was spent on funeral ceremonies and the feasts that followed, and so much gold and other valuables were thrown onto pyres or into graves, that various governments attempted to restrict such lavish displays. Plato, in the ideal world described in his *Republic*, proposed restricting the expenditure allowed for funerals to five *minae*, a large sum for the time.

In the Roman Empire, too, governments tried to limit spending on funerals, which were far more elaborate than those in Greece, especially since they involved tomb burials along the main roads outside city limits. The Romans employed a variety of funeral specialists; the word *funus* itself is Latin, referring to all activities from the time of death to the final post-burial ceremony. Overseeing all the arrangements was the chief undertaker, the *libitinarius*, who worked in a temple or grove of Libitina, goddess of corpses and funerals, where deaths were registered.

Supervised by the libitinarius were several mostly secular specialists. The *pollinctores*, who were often slaves, anointed the body and occasionally did some simple cavity embalming—replacement of the soft abdominal organs with embalming spices. The *designator* acted as master of ceremonies and director of the actual funeral procession, which included not only *singers* and professional mourners, but also sometimes *buffoons*, *jesters*, and *actors*, who imitated the deceased during the procession. *Torchbearers* also accompanied the procession, even after daytime burial became the norm. A *praeco*, or *crier*, was employed to announce the death to the town and to summon people to public funerals. For the rich and powerful, the *libitinarius* also handled the public ceremony, including a funeral oration. The *designator*—like a modern chief of protocol—had to deal with the sometimes ticklish questions of which people were allowed to walk closest to the body during the funeral procession. The *libitinarius*, *designator*, and *praeco* were free men, not slaves, but had low status in the Roman world; they were barred from politics while they remained in the undertaking profession, although some entered politics after retirement.

From ancient times, mourning in these Mediterranean cultures involved throwing dirt on the body and clothes, and tearing the skin and hair in grief. By Roman times dark colors, including deep red and purple, were clearly associated with death, and funeral specialists traditionally dressed in black. The Christians later forbade mourning garments, preferring to wear white as a symbol of immortality, but the dark colors eventually would win out; even in modern times, the religious robes worn at the funerals of important people are colored black, red, and purple. And many mourners follow the ancient tradition of wearing dark clothes to funerals.

Funerals varied by expense, and the different types were specified by state regulation. Elaborate funerals were held for the well-to-do. Poor people were generally carried out of the city on a cheap bier by a group of laborers called *vespilliones*, so-called because they performed their work at night, out of public sight. (*Vesper* means evening, or Evening Star.) The body itself was either burnt by *ustores* or buried directly in the earth by *fossores*, who dug the grave, often a communal pit.

To provide for a proper funeral, many Roman *artisans* and *traders* formed *burial clubs* to which they made a monthly contribution, in return for the club handling their funeral expenses. Such clubs also served social purposes and were the forerunners of the many later craft and trade guilds. *Soldiers* also put a small portion of their pay into a fund to provide for their burial or cremation expenses.

While cremation was a common Roman practice into the first century A.D., especially in the north, in the next two centuries entombment and earth burial gradually became the norm, even in the provinces. Outside Egypt, embalming was known, but rarely performed, except in special cases, being regarded as foreign and expensive. Alexander the Great was embalmed in Babylon, for example, and his mummified body was returned to Greece two years later. In 65 A.D., Nero's empress, Poppea, was embalmed before burial. Although embalming was performed in some parts of the Mediterranean outside Egypt at this time, it is unclear whether the embalmers were Egyptian immigrants or Greco-Roman *barber-surgeons*, who performed embalming as a sideline.

The later Romans placed their dead, over whose corpses gypsum was sometimes poured as a preservative, in elaborately carved sarcophagi (coffins) of marble, stone, terra cotta, lead, or wood; these were then put in chambers, in tombs, underground, or under mounds (tumuli). Jews in the Roman world had simple funerals, with no professional undertakers, only elderly women who laid out the corpses and professional mourners who joined the funeral procession. They generally placed their dead on shelves in underground *catacombs* alongside suburban roads. The early Christians did the same and sought refuge in these catacombs during their years of persecution, often building chapels there.

This close association with the dead led the Christians to make a major change in burial patterns. While earlier cultures had disposed of their dead outside city walls, the new Christians had no fear of the dead body. Because of their belief in eternal life and resurrection, they did not fear contamination or defilement from contact with the dead body. They even instituted the final "kiss of peace," which was administered to the dead by a priest. When Christianity was adopted as the official Roman religion in the fourth century, and the Christians moved their churches into the cities, they reversed the ancient separation of the living from the dead, and began to bury corpses within or next to the church. This move had enormous adverse consequences for public health for many centuries thereafter.

Under Constantine the Great, who made Christianity the official religion of the Roman world, the state assumed responsibility for burying the poor, providing a free coffin if needed. Laws were passed to prevent

Christ is laid in the tomb by family, friends, and followers, as was the practice in many cultures. (By Albrecht Dürer, c. 1500)

overcharging by the undertakers and their assistants. Gradually, however, the secular undertakers were bypassed altogether, and all funeral arrangements began to be handled through the Church. In contrast to the ostentatious, boisterous processions and wild lamenting of earlier funerals from Rome's "pagan" times, the Christians instituted a simple funeral style. The family and clergy washed and anointed the body, wrapped it in a white sheet, and brought it to the church, where the wake—the watch for signs of life in the corpse—was held. Mourning was private and even discouraged altogether. In place of the wailing dirges of the professional mourners, members of the Christian community sang psalms during the funeral procession.

Even the poorest Christian was to be given a burial with an appropriate procession, at minimum including a crossbearer, eight monks, and three other followers. The other special tasks involved in burials came to be performed by volunteers from among the Christian community. Notable among them were the *parabolani*, who tended the contagiously ill and bore their bodies for burial. These volunteers later evolved into a group of male *nurses* operating during the Middle Ages, especially during the great plagues. Overseers called *decani* supervised other Christians who prepared the procession, dug graves, carried coffins, and placed bodies in the ground or under stones within the church. From the fourth century A.D. onward, the Christian Church assumed full control of the burial process, laying down strict rules for the proper performance of all duties involved, which set the pattern for funerals in Europe for the next thousand years.

As Christianity spread throughout Europe, its funeral practices spread with it. Local practices gave way to the standard Christian burial centered, literally, on the church; Emperor Constantine himself was buried in a church. Later Roman emperors tried to reimpose restrictions on burial inside the city, fearing the attendant pollution. Other leaders, like Charlemagne in the eighth century, also tried to stamp out burials near habitations. All in vain, for the practice continued into the

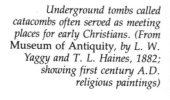

Underground tombs called catacombs often served as meeting places for early Christians. (From Museum of Antiquity, by L. W. Yaggy and T. L. Haines, 1882; showing first century A.D. religious paintings)

18th and 19th centuries in many European cities. When earth burials were forbidden, burials were made within the churches, which only compounded the problem, since the foul and pestilential fumes from decomposing bodies filled the chapels. Space within the church was limited, so that burial within the church walls became a privilege reserved for priests and powerful nobles, all others being buried in an adjoining churchyard.

These churchyards were used over and over; no attempt was made to preserve remains. After a period of several months to a year or two, the *gravedigger* would dig up the bones of the deceased and place them in a storehouse for bones, called an *ossuary*, re-using the grave for another corpse. It was because of this practice that the gravedigger in Shakespeare's *Hamlet* came upon the skull of Yorick, when digging a grave for Ophelia.

Gravediggers lived and worked in the centers of population; only in the period of the great plagues, especially the Black Death in the 14th century, which killed over a third of the population of Europe, did the gravediggers' work begin to move out of the cities. In that period, so many people died that the small churchyards could not accommodate them, and the first large suburban cemeteries came to be established. Even so, the pattern of churchyard burial continued, and the ground was so crowded that corpses did not even have time to decompose before the gravedigger had to disturb them for a fresh burial. In 1584, one observer said of St. Paul's churchyard in London: ". . . scarcely any grave could be made without corpses being laid open."

Gravediggers' work subjected them to some special pressures from parts of the population. Pieces of a dead person's clothing or body were held by many people to have magical power, so gravediggers, like *executioners*, were often bribed to provide such remnants. And, during those centuries when anatomical dissection was forbidden, some gravediggers made considerable extra money providing cadavers to experimenting *surgeons*.

Catacombs like these in Naples were magnets, first for tomb robbers and later for archaeologists and tourists. (From Diderot's Encyclopedia, *late 18th century)*

During the Middle Ages, undertaking functions, like so many other social tasks, were performed by members of the clergy, as adjuncts to their other activities. Even gravedigging was performed by a lesser church official, the *sexton*, whose other functions included care of the church grounds and bell ringing. Embalming, performed only rarely on important personages who were to lie in state after death, was the only funeral task still in the hands of lay practitioners, the barber-surgeons. Gradually, however, some funeral functions began to pass again from religious to secular hands.

Elaborate and costly funerals had been the rule for the noble and wealthy throughout the Middle Ages, with the expense and arrangements being handled by the state, church, or private family. But by the 14th and 15th centuries the rising middle classes also began to seek ostentatious funerals to suit—or more often to enhance—their new social status. The costs involved were considerable, including not only the burial arrangements, but also masses of draperies and other decorations for the home, great feasts, and mourning clothes, which were distributed free by the family of the deceased to all mourners at the funeral. A wide variety of tradespeople moved to provide this new range of goods and services. Many of those who developed an undertaking sideline were in the clothing trades, such as *upholsterers, drapers, cloakmakers, tailors*, and *glovemakers*, all of whom had been supplying items for distribution to mourners. *Chandlers*, too, moved into undertaking, since they supplied the large number of candles needed for the church burial, nighttime funeral processions, and feasts.

Lay organizations, formed originally as groups to pray for the dead or as trade guilds, also began to carry out undertaking functions. Such guilds pooled their members' resources to cover the heavy expenses of a funeral. When one of their number died, the steward of the guild then handled all the funeral details, including the funeral Mass, burial arrangements, payment of appropriate fees, and distribution of charity in the name of the deceased. He also arranged for a crier to make the rounds of the town, announcing the death and asking

In many cultures, as here in China, families offered propitiatory gifts for departed relatives, often hiring others to say prayers on their behalf. (From The New America and the Far East, *by G. Waldo Browne, 1901)*

the townspeople to pray for the deceased. In addition, the guild came to supply items that might advantageously be commonly owned, so as not to strain the deceased's estate.

Coffinmakers became important, as the practice of coffin burial revived. Throughout the Middle Ages, coffins had been rare, used only by the wealthy or important, and sometimes specifically reserved for them. For example, even in late 16th-century Sussex, England, coffin burial was allowed only to the families of the mayor and councilmen and to others obtaining a specific license from the mayor. But with the economic revival of the Renaissance, the practice spread to the middle classes. Although some of the very poor continued to be buried without a coffin, by the late 17th century coffins were in general use for most of the population. Even during the Great Plague of 1666 in London, most of the victims were buried in coffins, however hastily built. Many enterprising *cabinetmakers* or *joiners* took up coffinmaking as a sideline, and later expanded their line to offer other items necessary for funerals. As city populations expanded, and cemeteries were built farther away from the center of the city, foot processions gave way to horse-drawn hearses, and *livery-stable owners* were also drawn to take up undertaking.

This wide variety of tradespeople continued to operate with undertaking as a sideline until the 17th century. They were essentially *funeral furnishers*, supplying the necessary items required for the funeral, but neither embalming the body nor officiating at the funeral services. The funeral service remained centered on the Church, and the part-time undertaker generally worked out of a shop devoted to other activities. Most of these early undertakers were men, especially those from the building trades, but many, particularly in the clothing trades, were women, either working independently or carrying on a business with other family members. In many parts of Europe, women were generally brought in to wash and dress the body; sometimes these were nurses who had cared for the deceased during the final illness, but sometimes "laying out" was itself a specialty. In Germany, for example, the woman called in to wash and dress the body was given the title of *Todenfrau*.

As the continued concentration of population in the cities made specialties economic, many part-time functionaries gave up their former activities and began to work solely as *funeral undertakers*. The term *undertaker* had been in use for centuries as a general term for anyone engaging to perform any type of activity; but by the early 17th century, the term came to be associated primarily with funeral arrangements, and the undertaker emerged as a distinct occupational specialty. No special training was required for these undertakers; they needed only the capital, skill, or connections to provide all the necessaries for a proper funeral, and the ability to advertise their services.

In this period, also, undertakers began to carry out some rudimentary embalming. While knowledge of Egyptian embalming had never quite been lost, the techniques had been practiced only by some barber-surgeons.

Early undertakers, having no knowledge of either anatomy or embalming techniques, developed a very rough kind of embalming, replacing the soft organs of the body with a pitch and sawdust mixture. However unsatisfactory this must have been, public demand for such services was sufficient to attract to the undertaking trade a variety of other workers traditionally skilled with sharp instruments, including *butchers* and *metalsmiths*. Barber-surgeons protested vigorously against this breach of what they regarded as their exclusive right to carry out embalmings. On the continent of Europe, they largely carried their point, and modern European undertakers are still largely funeral furnishers, with any embalming being done only by specifically licensed surgeons, doctors, or professors of anatomy.

However, in England the decision went the other way. In London, in 1604, the barber-surgeons proclaimed the "openinge searing and imbalmeinge of dead corpses" to be their province, into which had intruded "Butchers Taylors Smythes Chaundlors and others of mecanicall trades unskillfull in Barbery and Surgery." The first funeral undertaker recorded as violating their monopoly was one Michael Makeland in 1646. But in the next two centuries, as the various medical specialties sorted themselves out into their modern divisions in England, embalming came to be practiced by the undertaker.

As the Europeans began to spread around the world, colonists took with them their burial practices. In much of Africa and Asia, where the colonial population remained relatively small and isolated in enclaves, these practices were applied only to the European population, having little influence on or from native practices. But in those areas where the European population became widespread and dominant, the funeral practices of the country as a whole came to reflect the practices of the colonists who settled there. So burials in South America tend to follow Spanish and Portuguese practices, while those in North America, South Africa, and Australia follow the practices of the northern Europeans who settled there.

Whether in enclaves or on sparsely settled frontiers, undertakers in these countries, like their earlier European counterparts, tended to be tradespeople, who performed a wide variety of functions in a small community, such as cabinet-making, livery services, or upholstering. In North America, many undertakers doubled as *coroners*, or worked as other municipal officials. But as settled metropolitan areas developed, undertaking emerged as a separate specialty in the colonial areas as well. In many areas, burial was initially in the charge of the sexton, who controlled burial permits for local churchyards, but as burial became secularized, many sextons also moved into undertaking. One of the first of these in North America was William Ensign, who in 1850 went through the New Jersey courts to establish his right to conduct burials in local churchyards.

In the 19th century, undertaking practices were sharply changed by the introduction of modern embalming practices. Scientists had first understood the circulatory system in the 17th century, when English *physiologist* William Harvey demonstrated the flow of blood by injecting fluids of different colors into a corpse's arteries. Shortly thereafter, other scientists, particularly Frederick R. Ruysch of the Netherlands, and Gabriel Clauderus of Germany, began to use arterial injections to prevent decomposition of cadavers being used in research. In the late 18th century, the Scottish scientist-brothers William and John Hunter brought to public attention arterial embalming as a means of preserving the body. While William wrote scientific reports on the technique, his brother John achieved public notoriety for the practice of embalming the body of a woman whose will specified that her husband could command her fortune only while her body was above-ground. (Once embalmed, her body was displayed in a glass case in her husband's house.) The increasing demand for embalming by the English and North Americans created a new type of undertaker, one who was not simply a funeral furnisher, but who possessed practical, scientific skills.

Arterial embalming was not immediately adopted as standard practice. Europeans were unmoved by the experiment and used embalming only for very special occasions, when the body of a famous person was to be displayed to the public before burial, or when a body had to be preserved for shipment. In England, the practice enjoyed some popularity, but was performed only on a minority of corpses. The technique was introduced to North America in the 1830's, being reported in some of the trade journals, which were newly formed to serve the emerging undertaking profession. At first there were widespread objections to embalming on the grounds that it involved mutilation of the body. But in North America, corpses were often shipped over long distances for burial at home, or were held in funeral homes for several days, even in extremely variable climates, while members of the family gathered from around the country for the funeral. Early undertakers had developed ingenious methods of packing corpses in ice to preserve them during these periods, but embalming was clearly a more effective preservative, and was enthusiastically adopted by undertakers. During the Civil War, too, the government hired undertakers under contract to embalm the bodies of slain soldiers for shipment home; the technique was used on Lincoln's son, Willie, and on Lincoln himself. As a result, the public came to accept embalming and the practice became standard, not only in the United States but in Canada as well.

Unlike the old pitch-and-sawdust cavity embalming practiced by earlier undertakers, arterial embalming required some specialized training. In America, the first formal course in embalming was taught in Cincinnati in 1882, in connection with a medical school. Such courses formed the basis for the later establishment of schools in *mortuary science*. Their graduates sometimes called themselves *morticians*. In the United States, embalmers are licensed and regulated by the individual states. In England, although an embalming institute was established in 1900, embalmers were not licensed until the 1950's, when the practice began to spread more widely throughout the country. In Europe, however, embalming continues to be performed rarely, often

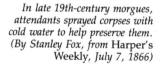

In late 19th-century morgues, attendants sprayed corpses with cold water to help preserve them. (By Stanley Fox, from Harper's Weekly, *July 7, 1866)*

requires a special permit, and is very expensive, being performed by a specially trained surgeon.

Another widespread change took place in undertaking in the 19th century. As undertakers became a distinct profession, their desire to increase their profits, combined with the social aspirations of their clientele, produced a trend toward ever more elaborate funerals. As in many earlier cultures, people often desired funerals that reflected a higher social status than the deceased had attained in life. Undertakers began to specialize in expensive funerals, with ornate hearses drawn by heavily plumed horses (which became used increasingly as cemeteries moved outside the center cities). Such funerals also featured ranks of uniformed attendants, the Anglo-Americans dressed in full formal attire including top hat, and the Continental Europeans wearing medieval-style black robes and hats or ornately decorated pseudo-military uniforms. During this same period, funerals tended to become secularized, with the ceremonies centered in the *funeral home*, rather than in a church or private home. This tendency was reinforced in North America by the practice of embalming, generally performed at the undertaker's quarters, and by the fact that the site of death was more often the hospital than the home in modern times.

The funeral furnisher has remained the standard type of undertaker operating in Europe. The handling of other death and burial functions, however, changed in modern times. The population growth of modern industrialized cities required some community controls relating to death, including certification of the cause of death; permits for burial, embalming, or cremation; and provision for burial space in suburbs outside cities or for crematoria. Functions such as these have in modern times been taken over by municipal or national authorities. While examinations, autopsies, and occasionally embalmings are carried out by surgeons, often specially licensed or certified for the purpose, the paperwork is generally in the hands of *clerks* or *bureaucrats* of little training and status. In many countries, the handling of the paperwork has become so burdensome that undertakers also have assumed the function of representing the family of the deceased in dealing with the bureaucracy.

State controls of the burial process came about in modern Europe for other reasons as well. In the 19th century, large undertaking monopolies established themselves in many parts of Europe, including Austria, France, and Spain. These firms, which often called themselves by some variation of the French *pompes funèbres*, offered elaborate and very expensive funerals to the wealthy. The less affluent, able to afford no better than a pauper's funeral in these areas, brought pressure on the governments, and in the late 19th and early 20th centuries, countries all across Europe passed legislation bringing the undertakers under government control. They did so in a wide variety of ways.

For large funerals, like this one for Admiral David Farragut, undertakers were absolutely essential to handle all the myriad of details. (By Theodore R. Davis, from Harper's Weekly, *October 15, 1870)*

In some countries, undertaking functions were taken over directly by the government. In others, the government fixed legal prices for funeral furnishing and services, broke up monopolies, and encouraged small private undertakers to set up shop. Many governments also set up government-owned crematoria, and took over or established municipal cemeteries. In many of these, graves are leased for varying periods of time, from a few years to "for the duration of the cemetery."

Funeral practices thereby became more streamlined and, with price controls in place, undertakers tended to drop the medieval-style black robes and hats or the elaborate uniforms of the staff, adopting instead simpler, sober dress clothing. The ornate old-style hearses and the horses, which required constant care and feeding, were also gradually replaced by automobiles as hearses; some of these were plain black, although others were elaborately decorated, imitating the horse-drawn hearses. Even after the advent of cars, in some countries undertakers maintained a small, horse-drawn white hearse for children's burials, later replaced by a white motorized hearse.

Modern European undertakers, although heavily restricted and controlled, still seldom require any special training, although courses in funeral undertaking are offered in various countries. Some European undertakers have formed national associations, and in various countries trade union activities have restricted the functions performed by various employees of undertakers. In Dublin, for example, *casket-makers* are not allowed to drive hearses.

Elsewhere in the world there developed no counterpart to the Western undertaker or *funeral director*. In most cultures, the burial process continued to be arranged and carried out by the family and local community. As in Europe before the rise of the modern undertaker, various people performed functions in the funeral process as a sideline: *carpenters* built coffins as part of their other work; *astrological advisers* counseled on the best time and place for burial; and *musicians* and *singers* played and sang dirges as hired mourners in the funeral procession. Only in the largest cities did these develop occasionally into specialties. Even gravedigging was often done by friends and relatives, although sometimes one person was selected within the community to perform that work.

In some parts of southwest Asia, however, there developed a separate group of workers whose job it was to dispose of the dead. In the Hindu and Zoroastrian cultures of India and Persia (now Iran), contact with the dead was regarded as a defilement, and the corpse bearers were a hereditary low class, shunned by society. In India, where cremation is common, their work involved bearing the body to the *ghats*, which were stone and concrete slabs on riverbanks designated for funeral pyres. Even in death, status distinctions were made, and the dead of each caste were normally borne by a corpse-bearer of the next lower class. In areas where wood was scarce, and cremation and coffin-burial unfeasible, bodies traditionally were cast into the water. Where fear of pollution or lack of water made that impossible, the bodies were exposed to the air, to be eaten by scavenging birds and animals and thereby returned to the earth.

In the Zoroastrian cultures of southwest Asia, air burial was carried out by a despised class of specialists; they bore the dead to remote stone towers, exposed the corpses to vultures, and periodically cleared the remaining bones into a central pit. No one but these specialists was allowed to touch the corpse after death or to enter the tower. The top of the tower was regarded as the most unclean place on earth; to go there, even the bearers wore special protective garments. Afterward, they performed elaborate purification rites, including washing with donkey urine.

Such specialists were not despised in all societies, however. In some parts of Africa, the *gravedigger* was held in awe, plied with handsome gifts, and entreated to "build a fine new house" for the dead person. In Tibet,

In India, bodies of the dead are burned on riverside stone staircases called ghats, *like this one on the Ganges River. (From* History of India, *by Fannie Roper Feudge, 1903)*

where the return of the dead is regarded as somewhat more natural, and contact with the corpse not defiling, the *corpse-bearer*'s work involved transporting the corpse to the remote hills, dismembering it, cutting off the flesh, grinding up the bones, and mixing them with grain to attract scavengers and hasten the return of the body to the elements. There a low-caste hereditary group called the *Tom-den* was responsible for disposing of the gentry, while other corpses were borne by members of the outcaste or pariah class.

In modern times, however, Western European burial practices have tended to be adopted in many areas of the world. At first this followed the pattern of colonial occupation, but more recently American-style funeral directing has been spreading throughout the world. While native and traditional burial practices continue in rural areas, the cities have tended to develop undertaking specialists, many of them funeral furnishers and increasingly funeral directors, who carry out embalming and direct all funeral operations. Because their business has made them prosperous, many undertakers have considerable status. Even so, the nature of their calling always sets them somewhat apart from others in their community.

For related occupations in other volumes of the series, see the following:

in *Artists and Artisans*:
  Furniture-Makers
  Painters
  Sculptors
in *Builders*:
  Carpenters
  Construction Laborers
  Masons
in *Clothiers*:
  Tailors and Dressmakers
in *Communicators*:
  Messengers and Couriers
in *Harvesters*:
  Gardeners
in *Healers* (forthcoming):
  Barbers
  Nurses
  Pharmacists
  Physicians and Surgeons
in *Leaders and Lawyers*:
  Police Officers
in Manufacturers and Miners (forthcoming):
  Metalsmiths
in *Performers and Players* (forthcoming):
  Actors
  Dancers
  Musicians
in *Restaurateurs and Innkeepers* (forthcoming):
  Butchers
in *Scholars and Priests* (forthcoming):
  Monks and Nuns
  Priests
in *Scientists and Technologists* (forthcoming):
  Astrologers
in *Warriors and Adventurers* (forthcoming):
  Prostitutes

Suggestions for Further Reading

For further information about the occupations in this family, you may wish to consult the books below or those in the General Bibliography at the end of the book.

General

Baxandall, Rosalyn, Linda Gordon and Susan Reverby. *America's Working Women: A Documentary History, 1600 to Present*. New York: Vintage, 1976. Includes some good pieces on householders and domestic servants.

Cunnington, Phillis, and Catherine Lucas. *Occupational Costume in England: From the 11th Century to 1914*. London: Adam & Charles Black, 1976. A fine book with excellent illustrations and much fascinating social history along the way.

George, M. Dorothy. *London Life in the Eighteenth Century*. New York: Capricorn, 1965. A picturesque view of common life in these times; touches on various aspects of social and personal services occupations.

Hammond, J.L., and Barbara Hammond. *The Town Labourer: The New Civilization, 1760-1832*. Garden City, New York: Anchor, 1968. A colorful look at the social conditions of the times with some special treatment of occupations related to the social and personal services.

Child Nurses

Ariès, Philippe. *Centuries of Childhood: A Social History of Family Life*. New York: Vintage, 1962. Translated by Robert Baldick. A classic in the field.

de Mause, Lloyd, ed. *The History of Childhood*. New York: Harper & Row, 1974. An interesting and readable account of childhood, with considerable material on wet nurses, midwives, nursemaids, nannies, and housewives.

Drivers and Movers

Boulton, W.H. *Pageant of Transport Through the Ages*. Salem, New Hampshire: Arno, 1976. A general work on the progress of transportation in history.

Stern, Walter M. *The Porters of London*. London: Longmans, Green, 1960. A thorough treatment of the portering profession in its greatest time—the 16th to 19th centuries.

Walker, Henry P. *The Wagonmasters: High Plains Freighting from the Earliest Days of the Santa Fe Trail to 1880*. Norman, Oklahoma: University of Oklahoma Press, 1968. A detailed study of this interesting subject.

White, John H., Jr. *Horsecars, Cablecars and Omnibuses.* New York: Dover, 1974. A good look at this special phase of the history of transportation.

Firefighters

Careers in Fire Departments and in Fire Prevention Work. Chicago: The Institute for Research, 1963. Outline of the job's basics, the routine, requirements, organization.

Dunshee, Kenneth Holcomb. *As You Pass By.* New York: Hastings House, 1952. Old New York, with many plates and some information about the fire companies.

Smith, Elmer E. *Firefighting at the Turn of the Century.* Lebanon, Pa.: Applied Arts Publishers, 1971. Solid information on equipment and techniques, with many illustrations.

Servants

Davidoff, Leonore, and Ruth Hawthorn. *A Day in the Life of a Victorian Domestic Servant.* London: George Allen & Unwin Ltd., 1976. A well-illustrated, brief, but evocative work.

Strasser, Susan. *Never Done: A History of American Housework.* New York: Pantheon, 1982. A voluminous, well-documented work concerning the effects of modern technology on the nature of household work, particularly related to housewives.

Sutherland, Daniel E. *Americans and Their Servants: Domestic Service in the United States from 1800 to 1920.* Baton Rouge: Louisiana State University Press, 1981. Interesting research showing how very important to the American way of life servants were in this period.

Swift, Jonathan. *Directions to Servants*. New York: Pantheon, 1964. A reproduction of Swift's 18th-century classic giving revealing advice to domestic servants and delightful insight into these occupations, with drawings by Joseph Low.

Social Workers

Hands, A.R. *Charities and Social Aid in Greece and Rome*. Ithaca, N.Y.: Cornell University Press, 1968. A classic work.

Lubove, Roy. *Professional Altruist: The Emergence of Social Work as a Career, 1880-1930*. New York: Atheneum, 1969. Useful on the modern period.

Walton, Ronald G. *Women in Social Work*. London: Routledge and Kegan Paul, 1975. A specialized work with useful detail.

Woodroofe, Kathleen. *From Charity to Social Work in England and the United States*. Toronto: University of Toronto Press, 1962. A basic overview.

Undertakers

Ariès, Philippe. *The Hour of Our Death*. New York: Knopf, 1980. Includes and supersedes his *Attitudes Toward Death: From the Middle Ages to the Present* (Johns Hopkins, 1974).

Farrell, James J. *Inventing the American Way of Death, 1830-1920*. Philadelphia: Temple University Press, 1980. Part of the American Civilization series.

Habenstein, Robert W., and William M. Lamers. *Funeral Customs the World Over*, revised edition. Milwaukee: Bulfin Printers, 1963. An unparalleled view.

————. *The History of American Funeral Directing*, revised edition. Milwaukee: Bulfin Printers, 1962. A standard work with much interesting detail.

Kurtz, Donna C. and John Boardman. *Greek Burial Customs*. Ithaca, New York: Cornell University Press, 1971. Part of the Aspects of Greek and Roman Life series. Focuses on archaeological evidence.

Leca, Ange-Pierre. *Egyptian Way of Death: Mummies and the Cult of the Immortal*. Garden City, New York: Doubleday, 1980. Translated by Louise Amal. A detailed account.

Mitford, Jessica. *The American Way of Death*. New York: Simon and Schuster, 1963. A modern exposé.

Rush, Alfred C. *Death and Burial in Christian Antiquity*. Washington, D.C.: The Catholic University of America Press, 1941. Part of the Studies in Christian Antiquity series. A specialized monograph.

Toynbee, J.M.C. *Death and Burial in the Roman World*. Ithaca, New York: Cornell University Press, 1971. Part of the Aspects of Greek and Roman Life series. Focuses on archaeological evidence.

Index

Addams, Jane, 137
Africa, funerals in, 170
Alberti, 11
Alewife, 114
Alexander the Great, 153,
    155-156
Aliens' Porters, 79, 86
Almoners, 144
Amber Route, 25
Amman, Jost, 4
Ancient Egypt, 26, 73
    ferriers, 24
    funeral arrange-
        ments, 148, 149-153
    servants, 108-109
Ancient Greece, 1, 93
    funeral arrange-
        ments, 153-154
    slaves, 74, 109-110
Andromache, 153-154
Animal handlers, 27
Anointers, 2
Antibiotics, 49
Anubis, 149
Apothecaries, 150
Armored car services, 43-
    44
Asia, caravans across, 26-
    27
Association for Improving
    Conditions of the
    Poor (AICP), 135
Astrologers, 63-64, 67,
    69

Babylonian wet nurses, 9
Babysitters, 19-21
Balia, 10-11
Barber-surgeons, 163-164
Barnett, Samuel, 136-137
Baths, public, 1-7, 103
Bearers, 30
Beasts of burden, 23, 26,
    38
Bergh, Henry, 143
Black Death, 94, 159
Boat operators, 23, 24-26
Bodyguards, 89, 92-92
Bolt, Thomas
The Book of Odes, 63
The Book of Trades, 4
Bottle feeding, 17, 18-19
Brakemen, 41
Brazillian porters, 81
Breton, Mme., 17
Bridges, 24
Brinks, 43
British Federation of
    Social Workers, 141
Bubonic plague, 94, 159
Building-maintenance
    supervisors, 104
Burial, 155, 156, 157-159,
    168-169
Bus service, 31, 41, 42
Butchers, 48, 94
Butlers, 113, 117, 121,
    125, 129

Cab drivers, 31, 42, 44
Cadavers, 165
Cadogan, William, 15
Caesar, Julius, 25
California Gold Rush, 37
Camel drivers, 23, 27
Canals, 38-39
Caravans, 26-27
Caretakers, 103
Cargo transport, 34-36
Carriage drivers, 34
Carriage, letters of, 77
Carro de boi, 40
Carters, 28, 77
Case conferences, 135
Castration: see Eunuchs
Catacombs, 156, 158
Central America, drivers
    in, 40
Chalmers, Thomas, 135
Chamberlain, 114
Chambermaids, 103, 117,
    120, 126
Chancellor, 113, 114
Chaplain, 113
Charabancs, 43
Charioteers, 23-24
Charity Organization
    Society (COS), 135-
    136, 139
Charity workers, 135
Charlemagne, 158
Charwomen, 118, 128
Chauffeurs, 44, 127

Chemical companies, 49-50
Child nurses, 9-22
  see also Wet nurses and
    wet nursing
Children's Employment
    Commission, 85
Children's maid, 117
Chimney-sweeps, 97-99
China, 26
  canal system, 25, 38
  cargo transport, 74
  matchmakers, 63, 64
  slaves, 74, 107-112
  transportation, 30,
    74-75, 80
Christian funeral
    arrangements, 156,
    157-159
City Porters Association
    of London, 79
Civil War, 125
Clauderus, Gabriel, 165
Clemens, Samuel: see
    Twain, Mark
Clerks, 113
Coachmen, 29, 117 121
Coffinmakers, 162
Coislin, Duc de, 118
Coit, Stanton, 137
Collectors, 136
Conductors, 41
Constantine the Great,
    156-157, 158
Cooks, 113, 117, 126
Coolies, 80
Coroners, 164
Corpse bearers, 153
Counselors, 68, 70-71
Cremation, 153, 155, 170
Criers, 154, 155
Custodians, 102

Dairy-maids, 117
Danube, 26
Dating agencies, 69-70
Datini, 11
Day cleaners, 128
Day-care centers, 19
Deacons and deaconesses,
    133-134, 135
Depilators, 2
Designators, 154, 155

Detectives, 89-92
  see also Investigators
d'Harcourt, Princess, 118
Diaper services, 62
Directions to Servants,
    117
Disease control, 96
  see also Sanitation
Dissectors, 149
Divorce counselors, 70-71
Dog catchers, 48, 49-50
Dolly-mops, 124
Domestic laborers, 107-131
Drivers, 23-45, 127
Dürer, Albrecht, 12
Dustmen, 100-101

Eastern matchmaking, 66-69
Egypt: see Ancient Egypt
Elizabeth, Queen of England,
    4
Embalming, 148 et seq.,
    155-156, 160, 163-
    164, 165-167
England
  baths, public, 4
  chimney-sweeps, 97-99
  country girls in the
    city, 121-122
  domestics, 121, 123-
    124, 129
  dustman, 100-101
  hackney carriages, 29
  labor unions, 79, 101
  London fire of 1666,
    51-52
  medical social workers,
    144
  nannies, 19
  nightmen, 96-97, 99
  police force, 89-90
  porters, 82-83, 84-85
  Red flag law, 39-40
  sanitation, 95
  stagecoach drivers, 36
  steam coach services,
    39
  watermen, 33
  wet nurses, 13
English Poor Law, 134, 145
English Temperance
    Society, 145
Enquirers, 136

Ensing, William, 164
Entombment, 155
Essay Upon Nursing and the
    Management of
    Children, 15
Eunuchs, 115
Euphrates, 26
Eurasia, ferriers in, 24
Europe, 10, 76-77, 134
  bathhouses, 3-4
  ferries, 25
  matchmakers, 64-65
  slave-servants, 112-113
Exterminators: see Pest
    controllers

Farmers, 78
Ferriers, 23, 24-26
Fielding, John, 123
Firefighters and
    firefighting, 33,
    41, 51-57
  porters, licensed, 82-
    83
Fleury, Abbé de, 118-119
Footmen, 39-40, 117, 120-
    121
Fossores, 154
France
  "Chinese" baths, 4
  drivers, 31
  firefighting, 54
  servants, 117-118
  sewer systems, 95
Franklin, Benjamin, 52
Friendly visiting, 133,
    134-135
Fullers, 59
Funerals, 162-163, 167-
    168, 169

Garbage collectors, 100-102
Gardeners, 121
Go-betweens: see
    Matchmakers
Godfrey's Cordial, 14
Gold-for-salt trade, 27
Gondoliers, 31-32
Gorgas, W.C., 49
Governess, 117
Gravediggers, 159-160
Great Plague of 1666, 162

Great Pyramid of Khufu, 73
Greece: see Ancient
    Greece
Grooms, 113, 117
Groundskeeper, 103
Guards, 89-92, 103, 113
Gurney, Goldsworthy, 39
Gymnasiums, 1, 6

Hackney carriages, 29
Hadrian, 2
Hamlet, 159
Hammam, 3
Hancock, Walter, 39
Harvey, William, 165
Hatshepsut, Queen of
    Egypt, 74
Haulers, 77
Hector, 153-154
Henry IV, 12
Hephaestus, 153
Herders, 23
Highwaymen, 28-29, 77
    see also Robbers
Hill, M. Davenport, 145
Hill, Octavia, 139
Hit men, 92
Holmes, Sherlock, 90
Homosexual activity, 6
Horses, 29, 42-43, 84
Hostlers, 26
Houseboys, 121
Household managers, 111-
    112, 128
Housekeepers, 103, 117,
    125
Housemaids, 10, 117
Hull House, 137
Hume, Dr., 14
Hunter, John, 165
Hunter, William, 165
Hurriers, 84-85
Hydrotheraphy, 6
Hygiene, personal, 4-5

Icemen, 85
*The Illustrated Weekly of
    India*, 69
Indenture, 134
India
    ferry operators, 24-25

funeral arrangements,
    170
matchmaking, 66, 68-69
Sardha Bill, 69
servants, 116
Innkeepers, 34, 78
Inquiry agents, 136
Inspectors, 139, 145
Insurance companies, 52
Investigators, 89-91
Iran: see Persia
Italy
    stagecoaches, 30
    Venice gondoliers, 31-
        32
    wet nurses, 10-11

Janitors, 102, 103-104
Japanese matchmaking, 67-
    68
Jewish burials, 156
Joubert, Laurent, 13

Kashmir, 81
Kher-hebs, 148
Knights, 89, 113

Labor unions, 79-80, 101
Lackeys, 117
Launderers, 59-62, 117
Letter of carriage, 77-78
Libitinarius, 154, 155
Life on the Mississippi,
    39
Lifeguards, 6
Lincoln Countess of, 13
Lincoln, Abraham, 166
Litter-bearers, 74-75
Loch, Charles, 144
Lock tenders, 39
Locomotive engineers, 40-
    41
London Guide, 36
Longshore workers, 86
Louis XIV, 118
Lucian, 153

Madames, 121-122
Magicians, 47
Mail transport, 3
Maintenance person, 103
Manchester, Earl of,

eulogy for second wife
    of, 13
Marriage brokers: see
    Matchmakers
Marriage bureaus, 68-69
Marriage counselors, 68,
    70
Marshal, 113
Marshall, Dr., 95-96
Mass transit, 42, 44
Massachusetts General
    Hospital, 144-145
Masseurs and masseuses, 2,
    5, 6
Matchmakers and
    matchmaking, 63-71
Matrons, 103
Mauriceau, François, 13
Mecca, pilgrimages to, 27
Merchants, 23
Messengers, 29
Michelangelo, 13
Middle Ages, 76-77, 160
Midwives, 10, 17, 63-64
Mines, 84-85
Missionaries, 145
Morticians, 166
Moslems, 3, 114-115
Mosquitoes, 49
Mother's helper, 19
Motorized vehicles, 85,
    101
Mourning, 155
    professional, 148, 153
Movers, 23, 73-88
    see also Porters
Mules: see Beasts of
    burden
Mummification, 150, 152

Nannies, 19, 20
Napoleon, 54
National Union of Public
    Employees, 101
Near Eastern matchmaking,
    63-64
Necropolises, 14, 151
Neighborhood Guild, 137
New York Times, 130
Nightmen, 96-97
Night-soil men, 95
Nile River, 26

Nursery school workers, 19, 20
Nurses: *see* Child nurses; Wet nurses and wet nursing

Obstetricians, 13
Oldenburg Hospital for Children, 19
One-day-a-week ladies, 128
Orphan girls, 122
Osiris, 148, 149
Ossuary, 159

Palaestrae, 1-2
Palmer, John, 36-37
Panama Canal, 38, 49
Pantler, 113
Parabolani, 158
Parole officers, 145
Paul, Vincent de: *see* Vincent, St.
Paving and Improvement Acts, 97
Paving Commissioners, 97
Peasant women, wet nursing by, 12
Perfumers, 2
Persia, funeral arrangements in, 170
Pest controllers, 47-50
Pimps, 121-122
Pinkerton's, 91-92
Pirates, river, 26
Plagues, 94, 159, 162
Plato, 109, 154
Pliny, 2
Police forces, 89-90
Pollinctores, 150, 154
Pony Express, 37
Poor Law Guardians, 145
Poorhouses, 134
Poppea, 156
Porters, 23, 73-74, 82, 117
  caravans, 81
  day laborers, 80
  fellowships, 79-80
  firefighting aids, 82-83
  horses as aids to, 84
  labor unions, 79-80

licensed, 82-83
London, 79, 82-83
mechanical aids, 85-86
organization, 83-84
see also Movers
Post stations, 30
Postal carriers, 76
Priests, 47, 63-64, 65
Probation officers, 145
Prostitutes and prostitution, 3, 121-123
Psychiatric social workers, 144-145
Psychology, rise of, 139-140
Pushers, 84-85

Race Relations Institutes Project on Domestic Workers, 130
Railroads and railroad engineers, 41, 42
Ramses II, Pharaoh of Egypt, 151
Ramses III, Pharaoh of Egypt, 152
Rat catchers, 47-48
"Red Heads," 54
Reed, Walter, 49
Refuse collectors, 100
Republic, 109, 154
Richmond, Mary, 139
Rickets, 16
Rickshaws, 30-31, 76
Roadhouse proprietors: *see* Innkeepers
Robbers, 2-3, 28-29, 37, 78
  see also Highwaymen
Rochefoucauld, Duc de La, 118
Roland, Mme., 16
Roman Empire
  baths, public, 1-2, 3
  charioteers, 24
  deaconesses, 133-134
  funeral arrangements, 154-158
  housewives, 111-112
  litter-bearers, 75
  sanitation, 94
  slaves, 74, 110-111

Rosenau, Nathaniel S., 139
Roulette, 30-31, 76
Russia, infant feeding in, 17, 18, 19
Ruysch, Frederick R., 165

Sallier III papyrus, 151
San Bernardino of Siena, 11
Sanitation and sanitation workers, 93-105
Sarcophagi, 156
Sardha Bill, 69
Saska, 17
Scavengers, 97
School-bus drivers, 42
Scribes, 113
Scullery maid, 60
Sedan chairs, 30, 74-75
"Seeing sessions," 68
Seneschal, 112
Servants, 11, 29, 107-131
Service-maids, 125
Settlement houses, 136-138
Seven Wonders of the World, 73
Sewall, Samuel, 16
Sewer cleaners, 101-102
Sexton, 160
Shakespeare, William, 149
Shiatsu, 6
Sisters of Charity, 134-135
Slavery, 11, 107-112, 114, 116, 125
Social Security Act, 140
Social workers, 133-146
Society for Organising Charitable Relief and Repressing Mendicity: *see* Charity Organization Society
Society for the Prevention of Cruelty to Animals, 143
Soldiers, 24, 89, 155
Soranus of Ephesus, 10
South African Domestic Workers Association, 130

South America, drivers in, 40
Spain, 3, 31
Spies, 68
Squires, 113
St. Lawrence River, 38
Stablemen, 29, 113, 121
Stagecoaches and drivers, 29-30, 34-36
Steamboats and coaches, 39-40
Stedman, John G., 15
Stewards, 112, 113-114, 117
Stewart, Miss, 144
Stews, 3-4
Street cleaning, 99, 101-102
Subways, 41
Suez Canal, 38
Superintendents, 103
Swift, Jonathan, 17, 120-121
Swimming, 5-6

Tacklehouse Porters, 79, 86
Teachers, 20
Team Drivers International, 41
Teamsters, 29, 41
Thames Tunnel, 41
Thermae, 1-2
Tibetan funeral arrangements, 170-171
Ticket porters, 79

Tigris, 26
Tollgate keepers, 38
Tomb chaplains, 148
Tom-den, 170
Torchbearers, 154
Toynbee Hall, 136-137
Trackers, 26
Tractor-trailers, 41
Trade, East-West, 28
Trade guilds, funeral arrangements made by, 161-162
Trains, 40-41
see also Railroads and railroad engineers
Transport firms, 34
Transportation, public, 29
Trolley car, 41
Truckers, 41, 44, 87
"Turkish bath," 3
Turkish cabs, 31
Tutoress, 117
Tutu, Leah, 130
Twain, Mark, 39

Undertakers, 147-172
see also Burial; Embalming
Union Fire Company, 52
United States
baths, public, 6
California Gold Rush, 37
motor bus service, 41
parcel post services, 37

servants, 123-124, 125-127
stagecoach drivers, 36-37
West, 37
University Settlement, 137
Usher, 113
Ustores, 155

Vespilliones, 155
Vetturini, 30
Vincent, St., 134-135

Wagoners, 34, 37
Waiting-maids, 117
Wardrobe keeper, 113
Watchmen, 89, 103
Water routes, 28
Watermen, 31-33
Welfare workers, 142
Wells Fargo and Company, 37
Wet nurses and wet nursing, 9-17
Wharfingers, 83
Window washers, 102
Workhouses, 134
World War I, 125-127
World War II, 126-127

Yangtze River, 26
Yellow fever, 49

Zoroastrian cultures, burial procedures of, 170

DATE DUE			